The GILDED AGE ON Connecticut's GOLD COAST

The GILDED AGE ON Connecticut's GOLD COAST

Transforming Greenwich, Stamford and Darien

MAGGIE GORDON

Published by The History Press
Charleston, SC 29403
www.historypress.net

Copyright © 2014 by Maggie Gordon
All rights reserved

Cover photos provided by the *Stamford Advocate* and *Greenwich Time*.

First published 2014

Manufactured in the United States

ISBN 978.1.62619.327.7

Library of Congress CIP data applied for.

Notice: The information in this book is true and complete to the best of our knowledge. It is offered without guarantee on the part of the author or The History Press. The author and The History Press disclaim all liability in connection with the use of this book.

All rights reserved. No part of this book may be reproduced or transmitted in any form whatsoever without prior written permission from the publisher except in the case of brief quotations embodied in critical articles and reviews.

*To Mom: I promise to always keep my promises.
Love. Never. Ends.*

Contents

Acknowledgements	9
1. In the Beginning	11
2. Railroads Bring Progress to Southwestern Connecticut	15
3. Wealthy New Yorkers Discover Greenwich	23
4. The Beginnings of Belle Haven	39
5. Old Greenwich Sees New Life	45
6. The "Captains of Industry" Stake Claim on Greenwich	51
7. A Gentleman's Estate at Conyers Farm	65
8. Stamford Sees Changes of Its Own	75
9. Stamford's Shippan Develops into a Seaside Resort	81
10. The Industrial Revolution Accelerates Growth in Stamford	97
11. Darien's Long Neck Point Comes into Its Own	103
12. The Legacy of William Ziegler	109
13. Tokeneke and Planned Development in Darien	113
14. The Day That Darien "Arrived"	119
15. The Gold Coast Transformed	123
Index	125
About the Author	127

Acknowledgements

Thanks first must go to my dad, whose moral support has never failed me. If it hadn't been for you, I never would have handed in my homework on time, let alone sat down to take on a project like this. Thank you for being you and teaching me how to be me.

There were several people who were instrumental in creating this book, and I'm grateful for all of you. First, I would like to extend a huge thank-you to Ron Marcus at the Stamford Historical Society, whose knowledge and generosity have been truly invaluable during this process. Additionally, I would like to thank my colleagues at the *Stamford Advocate* and *Greenwich Time* who allowed me to wade through the archives and offered up access to photos to help illustrate this book, as well as my editors, who let me divert my attention for a bit. Finally, I'd like to thank Sean Barrett for his encouragement and understanding throughout the several months of research and writing. I owe you a lobster dinner.

Chapter 1

IN THE BEGINNING

The area now known as Connecticut's Gold Coast, laced with beautiful homes and high-power residents, came from humble beginnings. But after the early settlement by Pilgrims and centuries as farmland, the arrival of passenger trains in the 1840s provided an unprecedented opportunity for growth and change, ushering in a wave of wealthy families from nearby Manhattan and changing this once provincial area into one of the most patrician parts of America.

The towns of Greenwich and Darien and the city of Stamford were first settled by Europeans in the 1640s, when men who had grown unhappy with the brand of Puritanism being practiced in the New Haven Colony searched for new grounds to begin their own settlements. Back then, the "Gold Coast" of Connecticut, as the area is now commonly referred to, was populated with tall trees and wildlife rather than the expansive mansions and perfectly manicured lawns often seen today.

In Greenwich, two Englishmen—Daniel Patrick and Robert Feake—purchased the land that would one day be known as Old Greenwich from Native American sachems for the price of twenty-five coats. This new settlement included all the land between the current Stamford border and the Asamuck stream in Binney Park.

While Greenwich is now and was mostly always a part of New England, Feake and Patrick quickly decided to place their land under Dutch authority in 1642. They had several motives for this move. Perhaps chief among these was the quest for seeking protection from the local Native Americans

The Gilded Age on Connecticut's Gold Coast

This 1933 sketch by Stamford artist Whitman Bailey shows a quiet afternoon in Binney Park. *Courtesy of the* Stamford Advocate.

and strengthening bonds between their settlement and the nearby island of Manhattan, which had been settled by the Dutch. Associating their settlement with the Dutch also helped Feake and Patrick—who did not include a church in their early settlement—further distance themselves from the arms of the New Haven Colony's Puritans. But this decision did not last long; by 1650, the land was again a part of New England.

While Feake and Patrick held the first deed for Greenwich land, they were not the first Englishmen in the area; Jeffrey Ferris and Robert Husted were also in Greenwich at the time. There were also other parties of families creating homes and settlements elsewhere in the southwest corner of Connecticut at that time.

In 1641, a group of twenty-nine families from the Puritan colony at Wethersfield, Connecticut, set out for a new home after disputes over land boundaries. Early that summer, these families crossed the wooden belly of Connecticut to reach the land that is now Stamford. Back then, the settlement included more than seventy square miles and stretched from Five Mile River—the present boundary between Norwalk and Stamford—to

Transforming Greenwich, Stamford and Darien

the Mianus River on the west, where the Greenwich settlement began. Its northern boundaries touched Pound Ridge and Bedford in New York State, while the southern portion extended down to the rocky shores of Long Island Sound and cost the "Men from Wethersfield," as they've come to be known, twelve coats, twelve hoes, twelve hatchets, twelve glasses, twelve knives, four kettles and four clusters of shells, which the Puritans used as currency.

It was only a few years later, in 1656, when the Stamford Puritans complained to New Haven's General Court that the settlers of neighboring Greenwich were being disorderly. The complaint alleged that the Greenwich settlers were entering into wrongful marriages and exhibiting lewd behavior, including excessive drunkenness. As a result of this complaint, Greenwich was placed under the Stamford colony's jurisdiction that year, an agreement that lasted nine years and stands as the only time Darien, Stamford and Greenwich were all one.

While Greenwich gained its independence from Stamford in 1665, shortly after the settlements had officially joined the Connecticut Colony, Darien did not receive its charter until 1820. The town's incorporation came to be after disputes with Norwalk settlers over timber cutting in the part of Stamford nearest to the Norwalk line. As a result of these issues, Thaddeus Bell filed a petition with the Connecticut General Assembly asking that Darien be incorporated as its own town. The petition was ratified in May, and in the official act incorporating Darien, the assembly set forth the date of "the Second Monday of June A.D. 1820" as the first town meeting, to be held at the Presbyterian Meeting House in town.

The name Darien was chosen by Bell, who surprised many who thought he would name the town Bellville, in honor of himself. But Bell chose Darien as the town's title because of its geographic location, according to The Corbin Document, a compilation of Darien town records put together in 1946 by former first selectman J. Benjamin Corbin. "He recalled to his mind the fact that two towns connecting two larger towns was an isthmus, in fact," Corbin wrote, adding that the Isthmus of Darien, which was located down in Panama, "was the only isthmus then the rage in the Western Hemisphere, and Bell thought that no better name could be procured. The new township was doing the work of the Isthmus of Darien, though on a much smaller scale, so the place was officially designated as the 'Town of Darien.'"

Over the coming decades and centuries, the three communities would each seek their own destiny, independent of the others. And while there are similarities in the stories of each, Connecticut towns are well known for their autonomy from one another.

The Gilded Age on Connecticut's Gold Coast

In Greenwich, additional land acquisitions, like the 1701 purchase of a large swath of property on the western shore of the Byram River, helped the community—then known as Horseneck—grow in size and strength. Farming became the way of life there, as Greenwich potatoes proved to be a viable commodity.

Stamford had a similar reliance on farming, though the town also has deep roots as an industrial center. After settlers established their own family farms, the community came together to erect a gristmill near the center of town, in the winding bends of the waters that now flow through Mill River Park. In 1651, Stamford's residents built their first barge, marking a significant milestone for the growing community.

"Ever since then Stamford has built boats, and carried on considerable water commerce," the late Louise Willis Snead wrote in "The Story of Stamford," published in 1916 as part of the official souvenir program for Stamford's 275th anniversary.

In Darien, life was relatively quiet, with business mostly taking place near its own gristmill, near Goodwives River, and trade centering on the inlet where Rings End Bridge now sits. Much of the business done in Stamford and Darien relied upon ships loading and unloading goods in their harbors during the early history of the towns. But by 1848, that was beginning to change.

Chapter 2

RAILROADS BRING PROGRESS TO SOUTHWESTERN CONNECTICUT

The first trains rolled into Fairfield County on Christmas Day 1848, carrying freight and passenger cars and forever changing the landscape of Stamford and it surrounding towns. It was another week before the New Haven Railroad line officially opened for business on January 1, 1849, when three daily trains began running between New Haven and New York City.

Before the trains came through, the first main route for transportation and trade in southwestern Connecticut was the Boston Post Road, a thoroughfare that still proves incredibly useful to the area. The road has a long history, originating from foot paths first created by Native Americans that were later connected when post riders began traveling between Boston and New York City in 1673. While the route proved efficient for the conveyance of mail, it contained long stretches of rough, rocky trails and was nearly impassable along several other spans. With these issues, the road stopped short of providing a means of movement for goods and supplies.

In the tercentenary edition of the *Stamford Advocate*, published in 1941, Stamford's daily newspaper writes, "Long distance freight movement was absolutely impossible. The charge in 1800 to haul a cord of wood twenty miles was three dollars; salt, one cent a pound at the shore, was six cents a pound 300 miles inland. With the beginning of manufacture on a large scale with the opening of new settlements inland, transportation requirements were far in excess of the facilities."

In addition to the Post Road, residents of Stamford, Darien and Greenwich relied heavily on the waters of the Long Island Sound to move

The Gilded Age on Connecticut's Gold Coast

Commuters await their train at the Stamford Railroad Station, which was built in 1868. *Courtesy of the* Stamford Advocate.

their products, first with schooners and sailboats and later with steamships, which brought crops to market in New York City.

It was in 1825 that Stamford harbor welcomed its first steamboat, the *Oliver Wolcott*, which made three trips to New York City every week for a charge of $0.50 cents a ride. That was significantly cheaper than the $2.00 fare charged by mail coaches, even after the coaches slashed prices to $1.50 in an effort to compete with the *Oliver Wolcott*.

But even the steamboat could not keep up with the trains clacking into town in the late 1840s. Railroads were an altogether new phenomenon then, the first American train having opened just eighteen years earlier on May 14, 1830. The fourteen-mile span, owned by the B&O Railroad, still relied on horses, and it was not until the following year that the first steam locomotive chugged over American tracks, connecting Albany and Schenectady, New York.

In Connecticut, the state legislature granted the first railroad charters in 1832, and the first railroad operation in the state made its inaugural trip five years later. This railroad, which provided service between Providence, Rhode Island, and Stonington, Connecticut, opened in November 1837 and forged a connection to the previously existing Boston & Providence Railroad. Other tracks opened one by one over the course of the next decade, connecting communities across the state with wheels of progress. These first routes had just one track each due to low traffic and the need to keep expenses at a minimum.

Transforming Greenwich, Stamford and Darien

The New York and New Haven Railroad received its charter in 1845 and was designed to run along a pathway from New York City to New Haven, the footprint of which is very similar to the route still used today. And while the first run took place on Christmas Day 1848, the train had to turn back to New Haven that first day when it reached Williams Bridge near the city after it was discovered that the Harlem connection had not yet been finished.

When trains first began connecting communities along the corridor bordering the Long Island Sound, rates ranged from $0.65 for first-class passengers traveling to New York City from Stamford to $0.70 from Darien and $1.50 from New Haven. But there were still considerable kinks in the system. For one, Connecticut laws did not allow trains to run through the state during hours of public worship, so trains were often halted at Port Chester, New York, for several hours before being allowed into Connecticut in intervals.

In her history for the 275th anniversary program of Stamford, Snead declared that no single influence "worked such 'miracles' as the coming of the locomotive with passengers in 1848, replacing the clumsy, lumbering stage-coaches on the public highway." She continued, "The railroad brought new people, new ideas, new methods, quick freight, and quick mails; in modern

A parade steps off at the intersection of Railroad Avenue and Greenwich Avenue in Greenwich, circa 1890. *Photo courtesy of the* Greenwich Time.

slang, it meant a 'boom.' New brick stores went up, so did land values; new churches were built, notably the Roman Catholic and Presbyterian. The humming wheels and hammers of industry were heard in the land."

While Snead's account was published almost a century ago, this point of view still rings true today. Ron Marcus, the current librarian at the Stamford Historical Society, said that "of all the things that have happened in 373 years in Stamford, the railroad coming into town is probably the most important," further noting that it opened up new avenues for trade while also shrinking the trip between Connecticut communities and the bustling center of Manhattan—opening up the possibility for people to commute from one area to the other on a regular basis.

The railroad brought more than just progress to the area; it also brought new residents. In the decade between 1850 and 1860, Stamford's population swelled by an additional 45 percent to more than seven thousand residents.

Just as new residents began flowing into the city's boundaries, many locals used the new transportation method to expand their horizons, as the daily trains into Manhattan made commuting much easier than it had been before. Of course, commuters didn't originate with the 1848 addition; several men had been living that lifestyle for years when the New Haven line came to town.

Stamford resident Albert Seely had been helping the city's commuters utilize the rails for seven years when the city's first train stop was unveiled in 1848. Beginning in 1841, he provided coaches for residents to White Plains across the state border in New York, where they could catch a train into Manhattan. But the events of 1848 made this kind of commuting much easier, and before long, demand for rail access was moving out from the city's center to neighborhoods farther north of the Post Road.

On July 4, 1868, a new spur line was opened, servicing the neighborhoods of Glenbrook and Springdale in northeastern Stamford, as well as Talmadge Hill and New Canaan stations, both located in the town of New Canaan, which borders Stamford on the east, just north of Darien.

Greenwich also received a great boom from the train. A 1990 special edition of the *Greenwich Time*, marking the town's 350th anniversary, states that Greenwich resident William Henry Mead was on board the inaugural train from Greenwich to New York City in 1848. And he was but one of a growing pack of notable men relying on the rails.

In the beginning, commuters were a limited population, though those who did hustle between Manhattan and Greenwich were among some of the town's most prominent citizens. The list of commuters included notable Greenwich

Transforming Greenwich, Stamford and Darien

This photo, taken around 1910, shows the intersection of Greenwich Avenue and Havemeyer Place in downtown Greenwich. *Photo courtesy of the* Greenwich Time.

residents like Robert M. Bruce, a businessman who had made a fortune in the cotton industry and later became one of Greenwich's greatest benefactors, donating the land that is now Bruce Park and building the original Greenwich Town Hall, Greenwich General Hospital and Bruce Museum. Eventually, the commuting ranks grew from a select few to a large enough population that more stations were demanded throughout the town of Greenwich.

In 1870, a new train station was added in Riverside. And though fewer than ten men hopped aboard the train each day in the beginning, a commanding group of landowners, captained by William B. Lockwood, in Old Greenwich demanded a stop in their neighborhood. The railroad company refused to create the town's third stop, arguing that the name "Old Greenwich" was too similar to Greenwich itself.

Not to be dissuaded, the residents decided to build their own station, financing it themselves. To sort out the issue of the name, the residents decided to change their neighborhood from Old Greenwich to Sound Beach, and they named their train station as such. The stop in their neighborhood was added in 1872, though it took seven more years for the station to be built.

The name Sound Beach remained for more than a half a century until a 1930 petition headed up by Edwin Binney's daughter Helen Binney Kitchel to revert back to the neighborhood's original name brought about a change of mind. Residents like Kitchel had become perturbed by an influx of

The Gilded Age on Connecticut's Gold Coast

In this 1930 drawing, Stamford artist Whitman Bailey depicts a summer day in Sound Beach, Connecticut. *Photo courtesy of the* Stamford Advocate.

visitors in the area, searching for a beach by the sound, as the name implied. But without any actual public beaches in Sound Beach, the misnomer had turned into more trouble than it was worth, and after a year of lobbying by Kitchel, the name was officially changed back to Old Greenwich.

With the rise of commuting, outsiders had easier access to the town, allowing them the opportunity to become acquainted with the area and appreciate all it had to offer. For savvy investors like New York real estate developer Jeremiah Atwater, it also provided the opportunity for large sums of money to be made. In 1865, shortly after the end of the Civil War, Atwater began buying large tracts of land, paying premium prices for parcels in the part of town near the Mianus River. Atwater purchased property, built homes and sold the newly developed pieces for a handsome profit.

In a 1935 book, *Greenwich Old & New*, Lydia Holland described Atwater's neighborhood, which he planned to name Riverside before meeting opposition from the government. His petition to name the neighborhood's post office Riverside, Connecticut, was originally refused because the small town of Oxford had recently applied to build a post office under that name. "On investigation it proved that there was no real reason for Oxford to make such a change, and it was persuaded to relinquish its new name," Holland wrote. "The petition was then accepted, and in 1869, Riverside came into being."

Within only a few years, Riverside became a bustling section of Greenwich and eventually opened one of Connecticut's first yacht clubs in 1888.

But just as the railroad opened up opportunities in Greenwich, it also posed problems.

Before 1848, Greenwich had been known far and wide for its fertile soil—despite its high volume of rocks beneath the surface—as well as opportunities for fishermen and the key location that allowed for easy shipping to New York.

And when the railroad shrieked into town in 1848, the excitement surging through the streets of Greenwich was not due to predictions of wealthy businessmen and their families snatching up premium properties and building Mediterranean mansions. No, it centered on a new, faster way to bring milk, potatoes and apples to the markets in New York City.

But while Greenwich farmers once cornered the New York potato market, the very railroad that offered express delivery of the crops also bolstered business for farmers in the Midwest, who didn't have to share their soil with large amounts of rocks and were therefore able to produce more potatoes per acre than Greenwich farmers. This new competition took a significant toll on the profits previously enjoyed by the town's farmers and traders.

As the economic viability of potato and apple farming shifted, Greenwich landowners had to find new ways to capitalize on their property. This is where the cosmopolitan newcomers found their entry point into the charming country town, as large parcels changed hands and purposes, from commercial farms to gentleman's estates, like that of E.C. Benedict on the shore or Conyers Farm in the backcountry.

As more and more people made their way toward the towns of Stamford, Greenwich and Darien, the single-track railroad system proved insufficient for the rising demands in the area, so in the 1890s, the railroad company expanded the route to four tracks. During this process, the rails were elevated and lowered at various points to eliminate the need for grade crossings. This allowed for trains to pass through the corridor with greater frequency, opening up opportunity for men to commute to New York City from the growing Connecticut communities.

Wealthy New Yorkers weren't the only new additions ushered into the area with the railroad's arrival. Hundreds of Irish immigrants flocked to Stamford looking for work, contributing to a massive increase in population by the time the 1850 census was conducted. By 1870, more than a quarter of the city's adult male population claimed an original hometown in Ireland. Census data

The Gilded Age on Connecticut's Gold Coast

Photo of the Greenwich Railroad Station taken before the third and fourth tracks were installed. *Photo courtesy of the* Greenwich Time.

shows that the town's population continued to surge upward in the coming decades, increasing by slightly more than 16 percent between 1870 and 1880 and another 39 percent in the decade between 1880 and 1890.

Greenwich experienced a similar growth after the railroad. In the decade between 1840 and 1850, the population swelled by about 28 percent, followed by an additional 30 percent in the following decade. The growth slowed in comparison to Stamford in the ten years between 1870 and 1880, when Greenwich grew by only 248 residents—a little more than 3 percent. But it picked up again between 1880 and 1890, when the numbers rose by 28 percent.

Growth came a bit slower to the town of Darien, which had only 1,705 residents in 1860. But as the land in this quiet town became a hot spot for development as the turn of the century crept up, Darien had its own boom. The town's population grew by 37 percent between 1890 and 1900 and another 27 percent the following decade—rates that exceeded the average national growth at that time.

In fact, Fairfield County as a whole grew far more rapidly than the rest of the nation between 1880 and 1920. During that time, Stamford's population more than tripled, going from 11,297 to 35,006. Greenwich's grew nearly as quickly, from 7,892 to 22,123, and Darien's more than doubled, outpacing the nation by going from 1,949 residents to 4,184.

And that was just the beginning.

Chapter 3
Wealthy New Yorkers Discover Greenwich

The promontory of land stretching into the waters at Indian Harbor in Greenwich is known today as one of the most beautiful pockets of property along the entire shore of the Long Island Sound. But the finger that has been home to some of the most elaborate and opulent structures seen along the sound's waters for more than 140 years was almost forgettable until its discovery by none other than New York's infamous "Boss" in the late 1800s.

William M. Tweed was born in New York City in 1823, the son of a chair maker. But the man who came to be known as "Boss" Tweed for his control of New York City's Democratic Party and who developed into one of American history's most corrupt politicians played a key role in the development of Greenwich.

After years of lining his own pockets (as well as those of his friends) with stolen public money, Tweed became a wealthy and well-known man. But it wasn't just his money that made him a household name. His shady dealings and dirty laundry were aired in living rooms across the nation when political cartoonist Thomas Nast began depicting Tweed as an insatiable aristocrat—plump and hungry—in the pages of *Harper's Weekly* beginning in 1869.

Soon, people in New York, as well as the rest of the nation, knew about the ways in which Tweed abused the power he had gained in New York City's Tammany Hall, skimming money off the top of public work projects throughout New York and thus increasing the cost for projects by five, ten and even one hundred times their actual cost.

The Gilded Age on Connecticut's Gold Coast

A portrait of William M. Tweed, often referred to as "Boss" Tweed for his role as the head of Tammany Hall. The corrupt politician was a well-known man around Greenwich, where he kept a summer residence for many years. *Courtesy of the Library of Congress.*

Tweed's money multiplied at a frantic pace, as he used the fortune he'd amassed for bribes to further his interests and to make significant real estate purchases. By the late 1860s, Tweed had bought up enough Manhattan property to be considered one of New York City's largest landowners.

But he did not limit himself to the island of Manhattan. Tweed's empire also extended north into Connecticut, where he purchased an estate in Greenwich. He found the quaint country community by chance. In 1860, a group of Tweed's Tammany Hall colleagues ran into bad weather while on a yachting expedition in the waters of the Long Island Sound and set up camp for a night on Greenwich's Round Island. When the yachtsmen returned to New York City the following day, they mentioned their makeshift campsite to Tweed, describing its serenity and noting that it would be a

The caption for this 1871 cartoon drawn by Thomas Nast and published in *Harper's Weekly* reads, "The 'brains' that achieved the Tammany victory at the Rochester Democratic Convention." *Courtesy of the Library of Congress.*

Transforming Greenwich, Stamford and Darien

A Tammany Hall outing at Boss Tweed's Americus Club on Indian Harbor in the late 1870s. *Photo courtesy of the* Greenwich Time.

nice setting for a summer retreat. Curiosity got the best of Tweed, who set out to inspect the island for himself, ultimately finding it much as his friends had described.

Tweed then gained permission from the island's owner, Oliver Mead, to use the land as a campground for weekend escapes. Then, in 1863, he built a clubhouse for the newly founded social establishment, the Americus Club of New York. The one hundred club members—most of whom were men associated with Tammany Hall—began spending idle days at the lavish Greenwich club, a place so ornate that an 1873 article in the *New York Times* argued that "few first class hotels in New York City can boast rooms with such rich and admirable appointments" and further described Tweed's suite of rooms, asserting that "it is doubtful whether those of the Emperor of Germany, in his country palaces are better furnished."

The Gilded Age on Connecticut's Gold Coast

This drawing of Boss Tweed's Americus Club on Indian Harbor in Greenwich was published in *Frank Leslie's Illustrated Newspaper* on August 12, 1871. *Photo courtesy of the Greenwich Time.*

The club building itself, designed in a large L-shaped formation and topped with a triumvirate of towers, was built on a cliff at what is now known as Indian Harbor. This desirable location gave the large white building vantage points that overlooked the Long Island Sound. The result was far-reaching and beautiful views of the water that only added to the extravagance of the building itself, which came to be known for its over-the-top opulence. "The floor is covered with the richest Axminster carpet, splendid gilded rose-wood escritoires and French plate-glass mirrors reaching from floor to ceiling line the walls on each side," the article states, further detailing black Italian marble mantels trimmed with rich bronze details, rosewood tables in the center of the parlor and a piano made available for anyone who may wish to play. At the other end of the parlor, a library "well supplied with elegantly-bound books which do not betray the marks of much use" was furnished with what the newspaper described as "the most luxurious and sleep-inducing chairs."

But the lavish club didn't satisfy Tweed's craving for a country estate. After becoming acquainted with Greenwich through the Americus Club, Tweed bought an eighty-acre plot of land from Greenwich Academy principal Philander Button for $18,000 and built a villa-style mansion, naming his estate Linwood. Tweed and his family spent weekends and summer downtime at this new country home in central Greenwich for more than a decade. The estate stood on the corner of Post Road and what is now Milbank Avenue, on the site where Jeremiah Milbank's palatial stone mansion, named simply Milbank, was built after purchasing the property from Tweed's wife for $475,000 in 1879.

Transforming Greenwich, Stamford and Darien

This drawing of Boss Tweed's Greenwich residence at the intersection of East Putnam and Milbank Avenues appeared in *Harper's Weekly*. *Photo courtesy of the* Greenwich Time.

While Tweed grew more and more notorious for his crooked ways in New York City, he came to be a well-known and even liked member of the Greenwich community during the two decades he spent time in town.

But the cracks in the foundation of Tammany Hall began splitting apart in 1871. That year, the *New York Times* effectively dismantled Tweed's empire, detailing his theft and wrongdoings in a series of daily articles that ran throughout the summer of 1871, prompting Tweed to transfer the ownership of many of his properties to his family members. He was eventually arrested, but even that couldn't hold down the king of New York corruption. After posting a $1 million bail, Tweed successfully won a reelection campaign for the New York State Senate that November. Shortly thereafter, another arrest forced him to step down from his office. With his bail leveled at $8 million the second time around, Tweed was unable to regain his freedom and died in prison in 1878 at the age of fifty-five.

Tweed's legacy in Greenwich is regarded as equal parts scandalous and fascinating. In the 1990 book *Greenwich, an Illustrated History*, published by the *Greenwich Time*, author William G. Harrington reminded readers that "the money with which [Tweed] was lavish was stolen money, every nickel of it, and that Tweed and his friends, who came here and established a hideout were criminals to a man. They made Greenwich, for a time, the laughingstock of America: the country town where the infamous grafter went out and threw around his money to buy respectability."

But the opulence of the Americus Club, where beds were dressed in blue silk and white lace and ornate furniture like tables made of "thousands of

The Gilded Age on Connecticut's Gold Coast

A photo of the original Indian Harbor Hotel before the annex was added. *Photo courtesy of the* Greenwich Time.

Children bathing off Round Island in the late nineteenth century with the Indian Harbor Hotel in the background. *Photo courtesy of the* Greenwich Time.

pieces of inlaid work," was just the beginning of a storied history of wealth on that particular plot of Greenwich land.

After Tweed's reign of Indian Harbor came to an end, his Americus Club became the sprawling Indian Harbor Hotel, which greeted guests spending summer holidays in the newly discovered resort town. The hotel was a popular spot for vacationers until 1895, when Elias Cornelius Benedict—another native New Yorker—bought the property.

Benedict amassed a sizable fortune on Wall Street during the latter part of the nineteenth century. But like Tweed, he claimed an upbringing far less charming than the life he grew into. He was born to a Presbyterian minister in the small upstate New York town of Somers. In his adult years, he remained connected to these humble beginnings by keeping in his possession a sermon his father once preached. The sermon had been written on the back of a bill from a shoemaker, since his father did not have enough money to write his script on new paper.

But Benedict created a new life for himself beginning at a very young age. He began his career on Wall Street at the age of fifteen and became a member of the New York Stock Exchange when he was only twenty-nine years old—leading him down a path that eventually made him one of New York's wealthiest businessmen.

Unlike many of the New Yorkers who flocked to Connecticut's Gold Coast in the late 1800s, Benedict was no stranger to Fairfield County. His mother, Mary Betts Lockwood Benedict, had local ties, and E.C. received part of his education in Westport. After earning his fortune, Benedict spent a significant amount of time on his yacht, cruising the waters of the Long Island Sound.

In fact, he came to be known as one of the world's leading yachtsmen and was known by many as Commodore E.C. Benedict. He was a member of six yacht clubs and succeeded William K. Vanderbilt Jr. as commodore at Seawanhaka Corinthians Yacht Club across the Sound in Oyster Bay. A stately man, with a full white beard and a cigar usually tucked into his mouth, Benedict looked just the part of a master mariner.

The well-traveled Benedict purchased the hotel and its property for $100,000 in the

Elias Cornelius Benedict was a famous yachtsman and Greenwich resident who amassed a fortune working on Wall Street in the latter half of the nineteenth century. *Courtesy of the Library of Congress.*

The Gilded Age on Connecticut's Gold Coast

The Indian Harbor Yacht Club as seen in the summer of 1897. *Courtesy of the Library of Congress.*

winter of 1895, ushering in a new chapter in Indian Harbor's history. The property measured roughly twenty-five acres and included Tweed Island, where one of Tweed's original clubhouses had been transformed into the Indian Harbor Yacht Club. After Benedict's purchase, the yacht club found a new location, and Benedict had the island leveled.

Benedict owned two yachts during his time living in Greenwich. His first was a 138-foot steamer yacht named the *Oneida*; years later, he upgraded to a 199-foot yacht, which he also named the *Oneida*. In his 1920 obituary, the *New York Times* reprinted quotes from an interview he'd granted years before, in which he said, "For many years I have kept a yacht and found that fresh air and sunshine are important factors in the prolonging of life."

At the time of his death, it was said that Benedict had sailed more than 275,000 miles on the smaller *Oneida*. Some of his favorite cruises included his several trips to the Amazon, where he had sailed more than 1,000 miles upstream, as well as trips to the West Indies and the Bahamas. Benedict often said he found the water to be relaxing, which is one of the reasons he purchased the peninsula property in Greenwich, where he could be surrounded by the calming waves even while on land.

In the few years after purchasing the Indian Harbor property, Benedict had a private lake built on the land to offer skating in the winter. In the spring, the lake was stocked with black bass, pickerel and other fish so that

E.C. Benedict's steam yacht *Oneida*, September 1895. *Courtesy of the Library of Congress.*

Benedict and his companions could enjoy fishing in the summertime. He also purchased several neighboring properties, buying out all the fishermen's houses near his gatehouse north of his land and leveling them in an effort to improve the aesthetics of his neighborhood.

This effort wasn't the first time Benedict had used his fortune to change the landscape surrounding one of his estates. Before purchasing the property at Indian Harbor, Benedict had a country estate at the top of Field Point Road and reportedly offered a nearby school $10,000 for a new gymnasium on the condition that the school would lower its roof, which was in danger of obstructing his view of the Long Island Sound.

In April 1900, a couple weeks before his daughter was to be married, Benedict purchased another sixteen acres of property adjoining Indian Harbor. At its peak, the Benedict estate totaled more than eighty acres, spanning the entire peninsula.

Benedict's estate was one of the largest and most impressive in all of Greenwich around the turn of the twentieth century, and its splendor has

The Gilded Age on Connecticut's Gold Coast

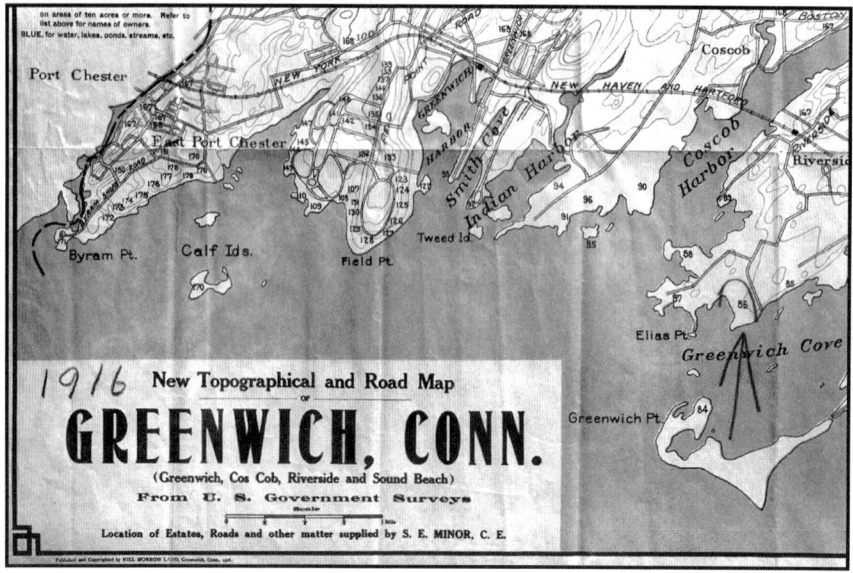

This 1916 map of Greenwich illustrates the town's harbors and points. *Courtesy of the Greenwich Time.*

been archived in great detail through an oral interview with Horace H. Bassett, a local dentist who spent his childhood roaming the estate where his father ran the staff of roughly two dozen household employees. At the age of seventy-two, during a 1977 interview with Richard W. Howell as part of the Greenwich Oral History project, Bassett recalled the exquisite touches he had marveled at as a boy. "Since then it's been divided up, of course, but at that time, it reached all the way from Bruce Park right out to the point and went completely out to Tweed's Island," he recounted in the interview, which is one of dozens catalogued in the 1970s—an invaluable local resource that provides a peek into life in Greenwich at different points in time.

A report in the *New York Times* detailing the April 1900 purchase also declared that it was generally understood that Benedict would purchase the property containing the Orchard Point Inn, a popular summer hotel that had been on the market for a decade. The property included 1,500 feet of water frontage and was expected to serve as the site for a mansion to be built for his beloved daughter's wedding present.

The wedding, which took place on April 30, 1900, marked a union between Helen R. Benedict and Thomas Hastings, of the world-renowned architectural firm Carrere & Hastings. With more than one thousand people in attendance, the ceremony was one of the largest social events of the decade in a town known for its high-profile celebrations.

The crowd was so large, in fact, that the ceremony had to be moved from the First Presbyterian Church, where the bride worshipped, to the Second Congregational Church, and a special train with eighteen coaches was secured to bring the guests to the ceremony.

The bride wore a diamond necklace and a white satin dress with a nine-foot train trimmed in lace and clutched a bouquet of rare orchids. After the formal ceremony, more than five hundred guests, including E.C. Benedict's close friend and former president Grover Cleveland, returned to the Indian Harbor estate for a celebration.

At that time, the groom had already won the honor of designing the New York Public Library. But his star continued to rise in the coming years, as he became one of the most prominent architects of the early twentieth century. His firm is credited with designing the Standard Oil Building and the interior of the Metropolitan Opera House in New York, as well as the Arlington Memorial Amphitheater in Washington, D.C., among other high-profile projects. Carrere & Hastings was also responsible for the design of Benedict's Indian Harbor estate, a distinction that set the mansion apart from other significant estates on Connecticut's Gold Coast.

The building's stucco walls rose three stories when the home was originally conceived (though decades later, a new owner would have the third story lopped off to shorten the building) and topped with a red terra-cotta roof. While easily spotted by sea, approaching by land was a different story. Visitors had to pass two gatehouses before reaching a five-hundred-foot wandering drive lined with oak, chestnut, walnut and birch trees that led to an elliptical entrance court lined with flowers and a grand staircase rising to the magnificent porte-cochère. "The first glimpse is most imposing," reads a 1902 *Country Life in America* article titled "Indian Harbor—The Ideal American Estate." "The house is of Italian renaissance. It springs from the highest point at the extreme end of the peninsula and is reached from the main approach by a long flight of granite steps, on either side of which a driveway sweeps in a half circle up to the porte-cochère. From this point a charming view of the grounds is obtained. Everywhere foliage has been massed to give a park-like effect," the article continues. "The stables, not far distant, are still so hidden by trees as to afford but a partial view of the roofs with the tall Spanish tower surmounting all." The article goes on to claim that the view from the water trumps that of the land, as the eyes catch a rambling antique Roman pergola, laced in honeysuckle, roses and grapes crowning the sea wall.

The Gilded Age on Connecticut's Gold Coast

Originally, the home, which was dubbed "the most conspicuous house in Greenwich" by the *Greenwich Graphic* in 1899, contained thirty rooms, and Bassett remembered riding in an elevator with six different stops as a boy. One of the most awe-inducing rooms of the home was the forty- by fifty-foot dining room, which took up the whole waterside front of the mansion's main floor, according to Bassett. The floor in that room was covered in a massive Oriental rug, and the ceiling was decorated in gold foil.

The drawing room, which could be found off the entrance hall, served as a place to entertain large groups of guests. The commodore was known to host annual concerts, for which he would bring up the Mendelssohn Glee Club from New York City on the *Oneida*. His concerts and parties came to be known as some of the most impressive in the whole town—Charlie Chaplin was even spotted there on one occasion.

While Carrere & Hastings created a new mansion in place of Tweed's previous club, some relics of Tweed's era carried into Benedict's ownership, including the old Americus Club dining hall, which Benedict had turned into what Bassett referred to as "the most gaudy boathouse you ever saw, because it was the old original dining hall with lights in the windows up overhead, and it was a curved, domed building."

As with most Carrere & Hastings properties, the landscaping and outbuildings were created in harmony with the main house. In lieu of open lawns, trees, rose beds and shrubbery were painstakingly planned and planted, leaving the tennis court to claim the largest stretch of virgin land.

In addition to the aesthetic plantings, the grounds also played host to vegetable plantings and livestock. The entire estate was mostly self-sufficient, containing everything from a windmill to an icehouse—a common occurrence for such grand estates, which were often home to dozens of staff members in addition to the owners' families.

"It had everything," according to Bassett. "They had a windmill, so it produced its own water. The food came from their gardens, and they had their own animals—pigs and cows—and so they got their milk and meat from the animals. He was self-sufficient; he didn't rely on the town for anything at all."

In the spring, the cows grazed in a field where wild onions grew, and their milk would carry the taste of onions, an oddity that left a bad taste in Bassett's mouth for decades. "If a cow grazes on wild onion, the flavor comes off in the milk," Bassett recalled in 1977. "We always got the milk and cream there. Always as we were growing children, Mother would have us drink a lot of milk, and it was terrible. We all hated that flavor of onions."

Oniony milk aside, the self-sustaining farm was a significant advantage for the Benedict estate. While most townsfolk back in the late 1800s had to worry about the delivery of their coal to keep the houses running through the winter, Benedict had a personal dock for the coal barge to unload at his estate. "They didn't even use the railroad. We'd see his yacht go down out of Indian Harbor," Bassett said.

Local recollections describe Benedict's morning commute by yacht to Manhattan, where he continued to work as an investor in his own brokerage firm until retiring at the age of eighty-three. Every morning at seven o'clock sharp, he hopped aboard his 138-foot steamer yacht, *Oneida*, offering a ride to any of his neighbors who also needed to be in the city. But seven o'clock meant seven o'clock, and in Benedict's eyes, being one minute late was no different than being an hour late. Once the *Oneida* pulled away from the dock, there was no turning back, and many a latecomer was left standing to watch the yacht swiftly steam away toward New York.

Much like its captain, the *Oneida* itself had a storied life. The ship played a key role in the secret operation of an American president in July 1893, when President Grover Cleveland, who was a close friend of Benedict's, was whisked aboard for emergency surgery.

On June 18, 1893, a Washington doctor examined a rough patch on the roof of fifty-six-year-old President Cleveland's mouth, finding an ulcer the size of a silver dollar, which one of the operating doctors later described as "extending from the molar teeth to within one-third of an inch of the middle line and encroaching slightly at the soft palate, and some diseased bone."

A pathologist, who was kept in the dark as to whom the patient was, examined a sample and determined it was likely to be malignant. When the president asked New York City doctor Joseph D. Bryant what he should do, Bryant

President Grover Cleveland underwent a secret surgery on the yacht of E.C. Benedict in the summer of 1893. *Courtesy of the Library of Congress.*

reportedly answered, "Were it in my mouth, I would have it removed at once."

But it wasn't that simple. America was in the middle of a political and financial crisis, centered on the debate to monetize silver. Cleveland adamantly supported repealing the Silver Clause of the Sherman Act to prevent further depleting the nation's gold reserves, which had shrunk significantly, causing economic turmoil. It was reported in several periodicals that Cleveland was all that stood between the United States and disaster.

In a 1917 account of the surgery, written for the *Saturday Evening Post* by Washington's Dr. W.W. Keen, Keen wrote that "had the seriousness of the operation on Mr. Cleveland become known earlier than it did, and before his evident good health put to rest the fears in the community and emboldened the sound-money men in Congress, the panic would have become a rout."

It was therefore determined that the operation had to be top secret, and Benedict's yacht *Oneida* was settled on for a location. After boarding the yacht in New York City on June 30, Cleveland passed the evening smoking a cigar and chatting on the deck of the boat where he had sailed more than fifty thousand miles with his good friend Benedict, becoming such a familiar face to the crew that they thought nothing of his presence.

During the surgery, doctors carefully removed a significant portion of the president's jaw without external incision to avoid scarring—a factor that helped keep the entire operation under wraps. Dr. Keen wrote of the operation, "The entire left upper jaw was removed, from the first bicuspid tooth to just beyond the last molar and nearly up to the middle line. The floor of the orbit—the cavity containing the eyeball—was not removed, as it had not yet been attached. A small portion of the soft palate was removed. This extensive operation was decided on because we found that the antrum—the large hollow cavity in the upper jaw—was partly filled by a gelatinous mass, evidently a sarcoma."

On July 5, the *Oneida* reached Gray Gables, Cleveland's summer home in Buzzards Bay, Massachusetts, where the president was able to walk to his shore-side cottage from the launch with ease. Twelve days later, after concerns that the operation had not removed all the affected tissue, the doctors re-boarded the *Oneida* in New York and picked up Cleveland in Buzzards Bay for a second, quicker operation. He was later fitted with an artificial jaw made of vulcanized rubber, which allowed him to speak clearly.

When word leaked to the press about a rumored surgery, the entire incident was downplayed, with the doctors refusing to comment and members of Cleveland's cabinet assuring the public that the speculation stemmed from nothing more than a toothache. The *Saturday Evening Post* story, written nine years after the president died, in 1908, was the first time the entire incident was acknowledged in full.

That particular page of American history is set on Benedict's first *Oneida* yacht, the 138-foot long steamer he kept at his Greenwich manse. But the second *Oneida*, which he purchased in 1913 for $100,000 (roughly $2.4 million in today's dollars), made history in its own way. The steel ship, which measured twenty-four feet wide at its extreme breadth and weighed more than 330 tons, was built in 1897 and cruised at a little bit faster than thirteen knots.

Benedict enjoyed the yacht for seven years before his death, setting out for a cruise to the Panama Canal only one month after purchasing the boat. Two years after Benedict's death, newspaper magnate William Randolph Hearst purchased the ship from Benedict's estate, and the *Oneida* was put to use for Hearst's International Film Service company. It was widely understood that the ship was meant to be used mostly for his mistress, the actress Marion Davies. Two years after purchasing the boat, silent film mogul Thomas Ince died aboard the yacht in a scandal that reverberated through Hollywood over the years. While it was officially reported that Ince died of a heart attack, Hollywood rumor and legend maintains that Hearst had shot him in a heated dispute over Davies.

The *Oneida* continued sailing open waters for several years after the Ince scandal, serving as a ferry on Lake Champlain after Hearst was finished with it. In 1940, its hull was sold as scrap metal, repurposed for ammunition in World War II.

Indian Harbor continues to be one of Greenwich's loveliest corners. While Benedict's original estate has seen a lot of changes in the last century, the magnificent mansion still graces the rocky shoreline.

Over the years, a string of renovations have changed the outward appearance of the home—including its being shortened to two stories. But the house is still striking from the water, where its majestic white face stands out from the plush trees (including a chestnut planted by President Cleveland a few years after his secret surgery) that have grown into maturity over the past century.

Even as multimillion-dollar mansions spring up around the home—many dotting land that had once belonged to Benedict, as the house now sits on about ten acres—it remains a crown jewel, dazzling boaters who travel past Greenwich's coastline.

Indian Harbor is just one of many fingers stretching into the sea from Greenwich. And while its story is interesting, it is hardly unique in the town

The Gilded Age on Connecticut's Gold Coast

of Greenwich. Just a few hundred yards away, separated by sound waters, lays the exclusive enclave of Belle Haven, a Greenwich neighborhood that owes its fame to a discovery similar to Indian Harbor's in the latter half of the nineteenth century.

Chapter 4

THE BEGINNINGS OF BELLE HAVEN

Belle Haven, a private association situated on a peninsula in southwestern Greenwich, hugged by the Long Island Sound, has evolved from a parcel of land where Native Americans kept their horses to one of America's most exclusive residential communities.

In the late nineteenth century, the Mead family—one of Greenwich's largest land-owning clans—purchased Belle Haven from the local Native Americans. In 1882, the land was broken up into smaller plots, and a year later, Belle Haven was incorporated as a community.

Evidence of Belle Haven's founders and developers can still be seen along Greenwich's picturesque waterfront, their legacies etched into the town's living history. Thomas Mayo, whose surname is now painted on street signs marking Belle Haven's Mayo Avenue, was among the first. As was Robert Bruce, who went on to become one of Greenwich's greatest benefactors, giving the town property for Bruce Park. Edmund C. Converse, who would later move to the backcountry, where he purchased thousands of acres, dubbed Conyers Farm (which, to this day, is one of Greenwich's most exclusive neighborhoods) was also among the first few to stake a claim on Belle Haven.

The community was developed as a "residential park," an exclusive area meant to be enjoyed by the well to do. The idea was common in the northeast in those days, with places like Tuxedo Park in nearby Orange County, New York, being developed around the same time as Belle Haven.

The Gilded Age on Connecticut's Gold Coast

This postcard of a home in Belle Haven was published by Mead's Stationery Store around the turn of the century. *Photo courtesy of the* Greenwich Time.

Sales in Belle Haven were slow at first, but after several years, a who's who list of residents transformed the formerly rural oasis into one of the East Coast's most prestigious neighborhoods.

In an oral history dictated in 1977, John D. Barrett Jr. described the enclave as it had been shortly after the turn of the twentieth century, when he spent his boyhood years in Belle Haven, first as a summer resident with roots in New York City and then as a permanent citizen. "Little by little, I would say mostly people from New York, Brooklyn, Brooklyn Heights and so forth bought the land here, which was very beautiful," Barrett said.

Trees were planted to line the roads, and magnificent gardens were planted by the residents, dotting the street throughout the area. There was perhaps none so lovely as the Italian garden grown on the property of Mr. and Mrs. Leo Martin, which boasted a gazebo, a teahouse and several statues.

But the lush green and pops of color blooming from flowers were only half of the beauty of Belle Haven. As out-of-towners bought up property in the neighborhood, they began erecting beautiful Victorian houses, like a parade of gingerbread mansions, sprinkled along the landscape. "There's a sort of style to some of these old houses, most of them built in the nineties," Barrett explained in 1977. "One thing they all have in common is a porte-cochère so that you could get in and out of your carriage without being in

The Belle Haven Casino shortly after the turn of the twentieth century. *Photo courtesy of the Greenwich Time.*

the rain. And a circular porch on the northwest corner of the house, no matter how it was built or oriented, so that in the heat of July and August there would be the northwest breeze."

While the architecture and the character of these Victorian "cottages" set the residential park apart from other country towns and communities in the late nineteenth century, Belle Haven's beauty ran deeper than porches and turrets wrapped in wooden siding.

The exclusive enclave of Belle Haven was more than ornate houses and gardens and street-side lamps illuminated by torch at night. It was a place to be—to relax and to be seen. So after the neighborhood was settled, residents created a club: the Belle Haven Casino, a magnificent building with a widow's walk perched atop it, providing views of the Long Island Sound.

Each year on Labor Day weekend, the casino would host a horse show as an end-of-season treat. The horses jumped and maneuvered through abbreviated hurdle courses on the casino's lawn as spectators clad in fine clothes sat watching. "It was all done with a great deal of ceremony," John David Barrett Jr.'s older sister Helen Barrett Lynch said in her own oral history interview. "I had a lace dress, which I seemed to wear every year for some time to the horse show. It was put away [afterward], and I was never allowed to wear it at any other time. It was made especially for me…black patent leather shoes, and socks, and the lace dress, all ruffles.

The Gilded Age on Connecticut's Gold Coast

A circa 1895 photo of Belle Haven. The former Americus Club building can be seen across the harbor in the background. *Photo courtesy of the* Greenwich Time.

And I had some sort of a weird hat on the top of my head. I can't tell you much about that, but I thought it was magnificent."

The casino was a social center mostly for Belle Haven's younger set, with tennis, boating and swimming commanding a large part of the daily lives of the community's youth. The bathhouse was quite unique looking for what it was, though it fit perfectly into the Belle Haven scenery, with gray shingles and turrets—a true Victorian.

Over the years, Belle Haven has been compared to other posh summer enclaves, being described as "the younger sister of Newport," at times. But in his oral history, John D. Barrett Jr. said he never thought of Belle Haven as a miniature version of Newport, saying that "it was a much simpler life" in Greenwich than the cliff-side cottages on the coast of Rhode Island.

Belle Haven came alive in the summertime in the 1890s and early 1900s. But come autumn, the shutters would close and the summer residents would trickle back to their permanent homes. "We came in the summer," Helen Barrett Lynch explained. "And in the early days, when I was a little girl...Belle Haven was shut up tight in winter. There were no lights. No one lived there at all, and the houses were boarded up."

The water and heat were turned off, and in many houses, like the Barretts' on Jack's Island, there were no furnaces to be found until the mid-1920s or early 1930s.

That was the lifecycle of a Belle Haven season in the early twentieth century, but as the decades sped along, the very nature of the community changed. For many years, the Barrett family shut up their home in late September or early October, the children commuting to school in New York City for the first couple weeks of the year before officially leaving Belle Haven. Then, around 1920, they turned their summer retreat on Jack's Island into a year-round home, and their father, John David Barrett, joined the ranks of Greenwich commuters riding the train into and out of Manhattan on a daily basis.

They weren't the only family to change their schedule; many of the wealthy New Yorkers who'd began taking up residences in the community for the summer months lengthened their stays until, eventually, they lived in Belle Haven full time. But while the residential park changed from a seasonal retreat to a year-round home, many aspects of the original Belle Haven plan remained the same.

Preserving the quiet life of the neighborhood has always been an important part of the very fabric of life in Belle Haven. In 1895, for instance, the

"Round Island as it appears in the artist's drawing was sketched from Rocky Neck Point," Stamford artist Whitman Bailey wrote about this drawing in the April 27, 1935 edition of the *Stamford Advocate*. He continued, "In early days, it was known as Great Island. It was then separated from the main land by sand bars that were completely hidden at high tide." *Courtesy of the* Stamford Advocate.

The Gilded Age on Connecticut's Gold Coast

town of Greenwich voted to buy Round Island, a ten-acre piece of land surrounded by water at high tide, for $75,000. But when Belle Haven residents opposed building a public park so close to their peaceful enclave, the deal was rejected. Later, Belle Haven and Byram residents joined forces to buy Calves Island, fearing the possibility of an amusement park being built on the island. In time, the residents donated the island to the town's YMCA—under the condition that no building visible from the north or west could ever be built there, in order to preserve the view from shore.

More than a century after Belle Haven was first developed, the neighborhood shows some marked changes. Back in 1977, John David Barrett Jr. noted that "very few of these houses are exactly as they used to be. Generations coming along, changing times, have altered to a new convenience in life, to the automobile, so forth."

And even more change has washed through the area since then. The fine Victorians and English Tudors of the late nineteenth and early twentieth century have mostly been remodeled or torn down to make way for new properties. The Belle Haven Casino has undergone a transformation and is now known as the Belle Haven Club, though it still serves a very similar purpose in the neighborhood. The club celebrated its 100th birthday on July 4, 1989.

The association is still home to wealthy families, many of whom earned their fortunes on Wall Street, just like the first Belle Haven settlers of the late nineteenth century, who were able to purchase their summer homes thanks in large part to the rich-friendly tax system that existed before graduated income tax was instituted in the twentieth century. But a cruise along the sound's waters shows a more modern world. Gone are the horses and the narrow streets lined with lamps, wood-shingled houses and the Victorian bathhouse. Today, the neighborhood's homes sell for several million dollars apiece.

Belle Haven wasn't the only beachfront neighborhood with beautiful estates sweeping into the sky. Old Greenwich is also well known as a desirable waterside community that rose to prominence during the Gilded Age.

Chapter 5

OLD GREENWICH SEES NEW LIFE

The history of Old Greenwich begins on July 18, 1640, when Robert Feake and Daniel Patrick purchased a mile-long stretch of beach from the local Natives. They renamed the land, then known as Monakewego, Elizabeth's Neck, after Feake's wife.

The 147-acre peninsula had a unique topography of open meadows, largely flooded at high tide, sending spans under water and isolating other areas as islands twice every day. Because of this difficulty, the property was still largely untouched in 1887 when New York financier J. Kennedy Tod began purchasing land in the area. After three years of smaller, strategic purchases, Tod came to own the entire point, naming his estate Innis Arden, a name that roughly translates to "high meadow" in Gaelic.

In an effort to correct the flooding, Tod constructed a causeway, built from rocks excavated in the construction of New York City's subway system. This provided a permanent land bridge between the two portions. The road, called Tod's Driftway, is now home to some of Old Greenwich's finest waterside homes.

Tod, who was born in Glasgow, Scotland, in 1852, was a golf enthusiast, and in addition to creating an enviable mansion on his Innis Arden estate, he also founded a 2,700-yard, nine-hole golf course bearing the same name.

The Innis Arden Golf Club was officially founded in November 1899, twelve years after Tod had begun working on the estate. He served as the first president, and other prominent Old Greenwich summer residents, like Edwin Binney and Edwin Lucas—the friend who'd arranged for the subway

The Gilded Age on Connecticut's Gold Coast

In 1937, Stamford artist Whitman Bailey drew this piece of the lake at Tod's Point, later writing in the *Advocate* that Greenwich's J. Kennedy Tod "must have noticed that the wild coast line of this entire promontory, with the waves of the Sound gently lapping its shores, and must have realized that the salt marshes and secluded inlets would always be a natural sanctuary for birds and other wild life." *Courtesy of the* Stamford Advocate.

stones to be shipped to Greenwich and later established the cottage colony now known as Lucas Point a stone's throw from Tod's estate—were among the charter coalition of sixty-four members.

To this day, Tod is remembered for his generous nature for several reasons, including his large contributions to the local fire department and other organizations. But he is most famous for opening up his golf course, as well as the rest of his grounds, for use by his neighbors. In an oral history collected by the Friends of the Greenwich Library, the late Mary Dodge Ficker, born in 1885, who spent her life living on Sound Beach Avenue, recalled that her family was among those with permission to use his beach, and they ventured there often.

The beach was admired for its privacy and the beautiful setting, as was the golf course. In a 1902 column in *Golf* magazine, the editor wrote, "There is certainly no golf course in the metropolitan district which can compare with Innis Arden for picturesqueness of surroundings. The Sound on one side, its blue waters dotted with white sails, the Cove on the other, with the general background of wooded hills and the green lawns of pretty suburban villas, all go to make up a picture that is not to be easily forgotten."

But over the years, visitors wore out their welcome at the lavish links. Local legend described an afternoon when Tod arrived at the first tee to find all the caddies engaged with other parties, making it impossible for him to play on his own course. And an April 1904 article in the *New York Times* declared that "too many summer boarders" drove Tod to revoke privileges from townsfolk and summer visitors: "As Sound Beach grew in popularity, Mr. Tod's golf course naturally appealed with greater force to the transient residents as a means of enjoyment. This constantly increasing number of players, combined with the fact that Mr. Tod believed his links were being advertised by some of the neighboring Summer resorts as an inducement to catch Summer tourists, have caused the owner to relinquish his former privileges."

Tod's friends understood and promptly formed a new club (which Tod joined) in a different location. For the rest of Tod's life, his estate, which had come to be known as Tod's Point, was a private escape for him and his wife, Maria, to enjoy.

Even without the golf course in operation, Innis Arden—situated on a hook of land reminiscent of a miniature Cape Cod—was a one-of-a-kind masterpiece. Tod's thirty-nine-room mansion was built into the eastern slope of a steep hill, and its front face featured high balconies perched atop the porte-cochère, looking out over a lake. There, at that front entrance, visitors first climbed six stairs before reaching the game room and taking an elevator up to the living room.

In total, the sprawling mansion contained twenty-two bedrooms, each decorated with carved mahogany or oak, and eleven bathrooms scattered throughout the house's many wings. In addition to the main house—as imposing as it was with five stories, turrets and a gabled roof—there were a dozen outbuildings on the grounds, including a carriage house equipped with a clock that is said to have rang out Scottish tunes like "Annie Laurie" at the top of the hour.

When Tod's wife died in 1939, the entire estate was donated to New York Presbyterian Hospital with the intent that it would be used as a convalescent home, something the Tod family thought it was well suited for because of its sun exposure and access to saltwater bathing. But the plan never came to fruition, and the hospital eventually found the upkeep of such a large property to be onerous. After leasing part of the beachfront for three years

The Gilded Age on Connecticut's Gold Coast

in the summers of 1942, '43 and '44—with the number of monthly visitors more than quadrupling to 72,000 between July 1943 and July 1944—the town of Greenwich voted in January 1945 to purchase the entire point and its islands from the hospital, creating Greenwich Point Park, which now draws more than 1 million total visitors each year.

While it may be true that Greenwich Point Park is considered to be the ultimate prize of Old Greenwich (and some argue the best retreat in all of coastal New England), the peninsula paradise is only a piece of a much larger community that grew from a quiet village into a popular summer destination in the latter half of the nineteenth and early twentieth centuries.

In her recollection, Ficker explained that when she first moved to Old Greenwich from Stamford in 1894 at the age of nine, the village was small and charming. At the grocery store, "we knew the grocer, and he knew you," she said. As changes swept through the community in the coming years, Ficker said Old Greenwich largely maintained its friendly feeling—even as she witnessed a shift in the very foundation of the neighborhood.

When asked what was responsible for the change, Ficker had a simple answer: "Oh, the summer people coming. They'd come up, you see, and hire a house or go to the hotel. Then they began to like it up here, and so where there were families, they bought a house for the summer. They didn't depend on renting; they bought summer houses. All the big houses around here were bought by city people."

The Edgewood Inn, pictured here in the early twentieth century, was a popular destination for summer tourists flocking to Greenwich. *Courtesy of the Library of Congress.*

Transforming Greenwich, Stamford and Darien

In addition to the posh new cottages going up around town, permanent residents who had called Old Greenwich home before the new wave of vacationers would also rent out their homes, either living "in little shacks in the backyard," as Ficker described, or collecting rent money to spend on their own leisure.

"Lots of people who had year-round houses used to make a good deal by renting their houses for the summer and going somewhere on vacation themselves," the late Harry S. Mortimer, who also grew up in Old Greenwich, recalled in an oral history of his own. "They could pay for their own vacation by renting their house out for the summer."

During the few years just after the turn of the century, Old Greenwich blossomed. A special dispatch published in the *New York Times* in May 1903 described the transformation in Sound Beach, as Old Greenwich was then called: "Five years ago this delightful resort on the Sound was known as a splendid place for raising strawberries. The Sound Beach berry had as much prestige as the Delaware peach has. Now the berry fields have been transformed into sites for cottages and the little farming hamlet has developed into one of the most flourishing resorts along the Sound."

The majority of summer residents took up cottages for the season, though there were two hotels in Sound Beach—the Kathmere Inn and the Greenwich Inn—both of which were also booked most nights during the summer. Both hotels offered tennis and swimming for their guests, and the summer residents who stayed in cottages would also use the Greenwich Inn for dinner and dancing throughout the season. Other accounts of the 1903 summer season show that the cottages were mostly filled that year and that both inns were at or near capacity for a large portion of the summer months. A July 11 dispatch in the same newspaper, with a dateline of "Sound Beach, Conn.," declared, "There is not a vacant cottage here now, and the Greenwich Inn and the other hotels are filled to overflowing."

It was a time of significant growth for Old Greenwich, according to Mortimer, who explained that it "grew in gobs because people bought up land and made it into developments. In the early days, there was a lot of vacant land down there."

Eventually, those newly built homes were being put to use for more than just the summer months. The cottages at Lucas Point, for example, were largely winterized in the coming years to accommodate a new breed of Old Greenwich townspeople, as wealthy visitors became permanent residents. The trend unfolded throughout Old Greenwich, Lucas Point, the Shorelands and elsewhere.

The Gilded Age on Connecticut's Gold Coast

"Living in Old Greenwich was every kid's dream because there was always so much to do at all times," said lifelong Old Greenwich resident Daniel Catanzaro, who was born in 1926 and grew up in a largely transformed town. "The people who lived in Old Greenwich were one big family. It didn't matter that I was a shoemaker's son or that you were the millionaire's son. We all played together, and we all were in and out of each other's house."

Old Greenwich residents came from a variety of backgrounds, as Catanzaro said, from workers to millionaires. And that economic diversity in town continued to increase throughout the latter portion of the nineteenth century and the early twentieth century, when some of America's wealthiest families came to stay in a community that, until just recently, had been a profitable place for potato farmers.

Chapter 6

THE "CAPTAINS OF INDUSTRY" STAKE CLAIM ON GREENWICH

In the late nineteenth and early twentieth centuries, America's so-called captains of industry rose to prominence across the nation, with families like the Rockefellers and Carnegies becoming household names. On Connecticut's Gold Coast, these famous families were also neighbors.

William Avery Rockefeller, an American financier who co-founded Standard Oil along with his brother John D. Rockefeller, amassing a large fortune, first began buying property in Greenwich in the 1870s.

A native of the small, rural town of Richford, New York, Rockefeller's 1922 obituary in the *New York Times* said that he entered the oil business in 1864, as a city directory in Cleveland listed one of his first business ventures with the line, "William Rockefeller & Co. Oil Merchants." Together with his brother, he formed Standard Oil in Cleveland in 1870, creating the foundation for what would become one of the world's wealthiest corporations. In time, he came to be known as the sphinx of American finance.

"Rockefeller branched out from the oil business and added untold millions to his fortune by becoming identified with various railroads and many public service corporations," his obituary continued. "He was a director in nearly forty of the country's biggest business enterprises at the time of his death."

While the Rockefeller family's fortune has never been calculated in full, it was widely accepted that at the time of his death, William Rockefeller was one of the richest men in the world. To many, he was chiefly known as "John D's brother," due in large part to the fact that he took great effort to stay out of the public eye. But as a member of a family who accumulated one of the

The Gilded Age on Connecticut's Gold Coast

This 1914 photo shows J.P. Morgan Jr. and his yacht, which he used to travel between his office in Manhattan and his summer home in Greenwich. *Courtesy of the Library of Congress.*

largest property holdings in Greenwich during the Gilded Age, Rockefeller became a well-known figure in the town.

Over the decades, he bought several parcels of land, creating a patchwork estate from previously unconnected pieces. His family's property eventually grew to more than four hundred acres, making the Rockefellers among the top landowners in Greenwich, something that didn't necessarily please everyone in a town overwhelmed with the growing pains of an agrarian society stretching into a new life as a playground for the wealthy.

In the late 1800s, wealthy men were able to enjoy and spend their money incredibly liberally. Money earned was money kept, due to a lack of income tax, allowing men like Rockefeller to buy up property and outfit it with luxurious buildings and touches with greater ease than most people have today. While the American government had tinkered with the idea of taxing income several times before—like the Revenue Act of 1862, which taxed income of more than $600 at a rate of 3 to 5 percent but was phased out after only a few years—it wasn't until 1913 that the Sixteenth Amendment was passed, ushering in the current system of taxing wages and earnings.

When Rockefeller purchased thirty-seven acres from David Husted, a descendant of one of Greenwich's original founding families, for $25,000 in the fall of 1903, the *New York Times* wrote that "Greenwich people generally deplore the sale, for it is another farm to lose its individuality in the large estate, as many others have done before."

It was the second time Rockefeller had purchased land from Husted. In 1880, Rockefeller paid $15,000 for a forty-three-acre plot, which he named Deer Park and turned into a sanctuary of lakes, brooks and open land with stables for horses.

William Rockefeller lived in Greenwich for several years but eventually moved to Tarrytown after disagreements about property taxes on his Greenwich land. While he changed his address, he continued to own the massive Greenwich estate before passing it on to his sons William G. Rockefeller and Percy Rockefeller, each of whom built a permanent home in central Greenwich.

William G. Rockefeller, the third child of William Rockefeller and the elder of the two sons, was born in 1870, about the same time that his father began collecting land in Greenwich. After attending Yale, he went to work in the family business, eventually becoming treasurer of the Standard Oil Company of New York, and in 1895 married Elsie Stillman, an heiress whose father was also a tycoon, serving as president of National City Bank.

The Gilded Age on Connecticut's Gold Coast

Accounts of the lavish wedding, held on a November afternoon in St. Bartholomew's Church in Manhattan, describe Elsie Stillman Rockefeller's dress as a princess-style white silk gown with appliquéd lace on the full skirt as well as the bodice and large sleeves. She wore a lace veil and a wreath of orange blossoms on her head and carried a bouquet of lilies of the valley and white orchids.

In addition to Rockefellers and Stillmans, the wedding party included financial magnate John Pierpont Morgan's daughter Annie T. Morgan, clad in a white silk gown, also trimmed with lace, and carrying a bouquet of pink roses. Accounts of the fête reported that the event drew a larger crowd of socially prominent families than Rockefeller functions had in previous generations, with members of the Morgan, Vanderbilt, Whitney and Astor families in attendance.

At first, the couple continued living in Manhattan, where they had both been raised, claiming an address on Madison Avenue, where the Stillman family had gifted them a home. But after a decade, William G. Rockefeller announced plans to renovate his father's home on Lake Avenue in Greenwich. He divided the house in half, separating the sections and inserting a three-story structure in its middle to create a roomier home suitable for full-time use by one of America's wealthiest families.

Even after this renovation, the home was considered modest for a man of Rockefeller's standing. The 1986 book *The Great Estates: Greenwich, Connecticut, 1880–1930*, assembled by the Junior League of Greenwich, describes the house as "comfortable, rather than elegant" and goes on to paint a picture of a house that was "in general, roomy and homey, with wallpapered plaster walls and comfortable furniture, not antiques but of good quality."

But the estate as a whole was expansive, containing everything a wealthy Gilded Age family may need, including a separate building for laundry, a three-story stable (which also housed two families of servants) and an outdoor tennis court, which was joined by a new indoor court for Elsie in 1930, eight years after her husband's death.

A 1900 *New York Times* article describing a newly acquired part of the Rockefeller property noted that the estate "commanded an extensive view of Long Island Sound, the Catskill Mountains and the lower end of the Green Mountain range," making the grounds a prize in their own right.

In many ways, the property was very unique, but it was also just one in a set of Rockefeller houses in town.

William's younger brother, Percy, also graduated from Yale and married into the Stillman family, wedding Elsie's sister Isabel. Like his brother's wedding six years earlier, the ceremony was a significant social event in the high-society circle. After a yearlong engagement, the couple was married in April 1901, also at St. Bartholomew Church in Manhattan.

The bride wore a creamy, white satin gown that was mostly plain but did have a few lace accents, complemented by her lace veil. The bridal party—with bridesmaids donning pink dresses and round hats decorated with silk, velvet ribbons and pink roses and each carrying a large bouquet of carnations—also read like a who's who list. Groomsmen included members of the Stillman family as well as Greenwich son James C. Greenway, whose grandfather, George Lauder, had co-founded Carnegie Steel along with his first-cousin Andrew Carnegie.

Brothers Percy and William had similar love stories, but their Greenwich estates could not be more different. A 1908 article from the *New York Times* noted that "William G. and Percy Rockefeller own adjacent residences which are in sharp contrast to each other. William G. Rockefeller lives in an old-fashioned farmhouse, and Percy Rockefeller in a sixty-four room mansion, said to be the finest in Fairfield County."

Percy's mansion, which cost $500,000 to construct in 1907 (roughly $12 million today), was the subject of much speculation as it was being built, including a substantial amount of interest in the unique heating and cooling features.

In an effort to ensure that the house was absolutely fireproof, the walls were constructed of more than eight hundred tons of hollow terra-cotta blocks, with not a stitch of wood used in the construction. The eight-inch-thick wall of hollow blocks on the outside was separated from a second four-inch-thick wall by a four-inch gap, creating a confined air space in between, which helped keep the house warmer in the winter and cooler in the summer.

The exterior was covered in stucco, while the terra-cotta interior was covered with plaster. When it was complete, the sprawling mansion contained more than sixty rooms, including ten bathrooms and more than a dozen servants' rooms. The League's book provides a description of a few of the rooms in an effort to "give some idea of the grandeur" of the mansion: "The library was some sixty feet long and about half as wide, finished in dark, weathered oak with bookshelves of the same material built into the walls. The ceilings were paneled and hand-decorated. At either end were huge fireplaces with exquisitely carved Cannes marble mantelpieces. Most of the other rooms were finished in cherry wood enameled in white. There were other fireplaces of French and Italian marble and some unusually intricate oak carvings. Floors were of fine hardwood." The book goes on to detail a $700 white metal sink in one of the kitchens. In today's dollars, that bill would register at more than $16,000.

The Gilded Age on Connecticut's Gold Coast

In 1923, Percy Rockefeller was the third-largest taxpayer in the town of Greenwich in terms of real estate, with an assessment of $675,950 worth of property, or $9.24 million in today's dollars. That same year, his brother William's estate had the fifth-highest taxes in towns, being assessed at $546,383, or $7.47 million in today's currency.

But both Rockefeller homes were torn down in the 1930s, as changing tastes and the beginning of America's Great Depression rendered great estates like these impractical and dated. The ornate trappings at Percy Rockefeller's Owenoke Farm were auctioned off, sending Oriental rugs and antique walnut furniture out of the house, which was destroyed with dynamite. Though neither home survived, the Rockefellers' real estate legacy in Greenwich was far from over.

James Stillman Rockefeller, son of William G. Rockefeller, grew up in the farmhouse on Lake Avenue along with his four siblings. Like his father, James attended Yale University, where he captained the crew team. In 1924, the same year he graduated, his team went on to win a gold medal at the Olympic games in Paris, landing his portrait on the cover of *Time* magazine. A year later, he married Andrew Carnegie's niece, Nancy Carnegie, and in 1929, he built a mansion of his own on the family estate, where he and his wife lived for many decades.

Having already been born into a vast fortune, James Stillman Rockefeller worked to become a prominent businessman in his own right, eventually serving as president and, later, chairman of Citigroup. He died of a stroke in 2004 at the age of 102 after a long life of business and philanthropy. The Rockfield estate, which was home to the nineteen-thousand-square-foot brick Georgian mansion he'd constructed eighty years earlier, was sold out of the Rockefeller family three years after his death for $13.7 million.

Just two years later, after extensive remodeling and renovating, the house changed hands again, commanding $22.5 million. At that time, the mansion boasted a dozen fireplaces, eleven bedrooms and sixteen bathrooms and was situated on more than eleven acres, complete with traditional English gardens. After spending less than three weeks on the real estate market, the sale was considered to be exceptionally quick during a recession that greatly slowed the Greenwich real estate market in 2009.

The real estate listing touted Rockfield as possessing "old-world elegance and majesty with every modern amenity" throughout its four stories, including high ceilings, antique floors and original moldings. Trumpeting historic touches like a mahogany billiard room and a paneled library in the same home as modern luxury mainstays like a theater, gym and pool, the

Transforming Greenwich, Stamford and Darien

listing boasted that the property provided "an unprecedented opportunity for the discerning buyer to own a piece of Greenwich history."

The house still stands as an example of Greenwich's Gilded Age and as one of several reminders of the Rockefellers' holdings, which swelled to more than five hundred acres over scores of years of acquisition and development.

And it's not the only lasting impression the Rockefellers left on that particular part of Greenwich. Their vast holdings are now the home of Deer Park, a forty-three-acre planned community that contains many homes like Rockfield. Plots from the Rockefellers' large tract of land were sold off methodically, with zoning restrictions that pre-dated the town of Greenwich's own laws, resulting in a well-planned mid-country neighborhood that is now home to a swath of beautiful estates situated on large lawns.

When chronicling the stories of America's captains of industry around the turn of the twentieth century, the Rockefeller family is often mentioned in the same breath as the Carnegies and the Vanderbilts. And the latter two families also have several interesting ties to Connecticut's Gold Coast.

At the age of sixty-six, Andrew Carnegie was already one of the wealthiest men in the nation, having earned his fortune in oil, railroads and metal, when his Carnegie Steel Company was bought out by J.P. Morgan in 1901 for $480 million (more than $11 billion in today's dollars), creating the foundation for Morgan's U.S. Steel Company.

After his retirement that year, the native Scot, who had amassed his empire in Pittsburgh, spent several summers at a vacation home on Long Neck Point in Darien. The brick home, situated on a nine-acre lot at the very tip of Long Neck Point—a quiet and peaceful peninsula that jutted farther out into the Long Island Sound than any of the neighboring necks—belonged to Anson Phelps Stokes, a New York native born in 1838 who became a multimillionaire through mining and railroad operations, among other things.

Stokes was part of New York's high-society circle, his name being included on guest lists of the era's premiere social events, such as J.P. Morgan's eldest daughter's wedding in 1900. In addition to his property in Darien—which would later become the home of the Convent of the Sacred Heart—Stokes also claimed a "cottage" in Lenox, Massachusetts. His home there, dubbed Shadow Brook, was the largest Lenox home of its time when it was completed in 1894 at an estimated total cost of $1 million.

Shadow Brook was part of a total estate that grew to nine hundred acres of land on the shores of Mahkeenac Lake, a couple miles west of the village of Lenox. The cottage contained more than one hundred rooms, leading to

The Gilded Age on Connecticut's Gold Coast

A postcard of the brick house at the end of Collender's Point in Darien, where Andrew Carnegie once spent a summer. *Photo courtesy of the* Darien News.

claims that it was one of the largest country houses in America, stretching more than four hundred feet in length. With a first floor constructed of marble, second and third floors done in stucco and timber in the old English tradition and a red-tiled roof, the home was a sight to be seen. And Andrew Carnegie has ties to that estate as well.

The very same *New York Times* article that mentions Carnegie staying at the Stokes's Long Neck Point property in the summer of 1916 details the $350,000 purchase of Shadow Brook by the Carnegie family: "Mr. Carnegie has been at Noroton, Conn, at the country place of Mrs. Anson Phelps Stokes, the last season. His health has been poor. A report in Lenox is that physicians advised a higher altitude, and the Shadow Brook property was decided upon for the reason of its being isolated."

At the time of Carnegie's purchase, Stokes had already passed away, having died in 1913 at the age of seventy-five. The Stokes family sold the home to a family from Georgia in 1904, and in 1915, the summer before Carnegie made his purchase, Margaret Vanderbilt, widow of Andrew Vanderbilt, who died in the sinking of the *Lusitania* earlier that year, spent the summer there.

The Stokes family had other considerable real estate holdings in this corner of Connecticut. Anson Phelps Stokes's son Isaac Newton Phelps Stokes grew up to become a noted architect, responsible for designing St. Paul's Chapel at Columbia University, among other well-known buildings on Ivy League campuses throughout the Northeast. But his contribution to

Transforming Greenwich, Stamford and Darien

Greenwich centered on the unique estate he built in the town's mid-country, which he named Khakum Wood.

An 1891 graduate of Harvard University, Stokes married Edith Minturn, daughter of the late shipping heir Robert B. Minturn, in 1895 in Quebec. Five years later, the couple bought just over 175 acres of land that, like the Rockefeller purchases, had originally been owned by the Husted family. Stokes served as his own architect for the house he planned on the property and began building a Tudor-style manor home five years after making the purchase, adding an octagonal tower two years later.

Then, in the summer of 1910, he stumbled upon an advertisement in *English Country Life* magazine offering up the materials for a sixteenth-century Tudor home called the High-Low House. Stokes jumped at the opportunity to purchase the material. He had the house disassembled at its original location, packed into more than 650 crates and shipped across the Atlantic to be reassembled on his Khakum Wood estate in Greenwich.

Over the course of several months, a team of more than a dozen craftsmen painstakingly reassembled the house, affixing it to the two existing sections of Stokes's house. As a result, the finished home, which Stokes called High-Low House (just as it had been named in its original location in Suffolk, England) was "the oldest-occupied house in the United States in 1912" when it was completed, according to the Junior League's book, which described the final product as a harmonious union of both parts: "The old manor house stood as it had in England, each timber, tile, and chimney brick in its original place, preserving all the mellowness and irregularities that come only with age. The weathered red-tiled roof and the soft tones of the aged wood and brickwork contrasted yet blended with the gray stone of the main body of the house to which it had been skillfully connected as a wing."

While playing host to the nation's oldest dwelling was certainly notable, the estate's gardens were equally interesting. They were designed by Frederick Law Olmstead Jr., a Boston-based landscape architect whose portfolio included design projects at the National Mall, the White House grounds, the Jefferson Memorial and the grounds of George Vanderbilt's Biltmore Estate in North Carolina, which was the nation's largest private residence. Olmstead trained with his father, who had earned fame designing New York City's Central Park in the 1850s.

In fact, it was the grounds at Khakum Wood that truly stood the test of time. In 1925, Stokes began selling plots from his 177-acre estate as part of a plan he had developed with the help of Olmstead. The plan aimed to create an exclusive and restricted residential development on the grounds, similar

The Gilded Age on Connecticut's Gold Coast

to the Rockefeller plan at Deer Park. The Khakum Wood Association was officially incorporated in June 1929 and still exists today.

In 1937, when his wife, Edith, died, Stokes had already successfully sold thirty plots, with another dozen ready to go. They ranged in size from 2 to 7 acres and offered town water as well as underground utilities. By the time the sales were complete, the 155-acre subdivision was known to be one of the finest residential associations in Greenwich.

Stokes's High-Low House was torn down shortly after his death in 1944 to make way for a more modern home, but the exclusive enclave of estate homes he created has become an integral part of Greenwich's landscape over the years.

While the name may not carry the same recognition as Rockefeller or Carnegie, a list of turn-of-the-century power families who left an indelible impression on the towns of Stamford, Greenwich and Darien would not be complete without mentioning the Lauder and Greenway families, who owned a sprawling property on the Long Island Sound.

The original brownstone, named Kincraig, was built in the 1890s by New York City native John Hamilton Gourlie, an insurance expert and author. Gourlie had been one of the original New Yorkers to develop and settle in Belle Haven, where he built a pair of cottages in which he barely lived. According to his obituary in the *New York Times*, Gourlie had "declared he was wealthy enough" without having to rent out his properties.

In 1893, Gourlie purchased an estate in Mead's Point, a shoreline spot near Belle Haven, situated at the mouth of the Mianus River. He built a mansion on the virgin property, directly across Indian Harbor from E.C. Benedict's home, and he lived there for seven years before moving on to travel abroad to Egypt and remarry his nurse.

After Gourlie passed away in 1904 at the age of fifty-one, leaving no will, his heirs sold the property to Harriet Lauder Greenway, a daughter of millionaire George Lauder, who co-founded the Carnegie Steel Company in Pittsburgh along with Harriet's uncle Andrew Carnegie. Harriet Lauder had married James Greenway of New York City in 1902 after a three-year courtship that began when the pair met after a Yale-Princeton football game, in which Greenway had played tackle for Yale. As a wedding gift, Andrew Carnegie gave his niece $1 million, which likely helped finance the Greenwich purchase years later.

When the Lauder-Greenway family purchased the Gourlie property, it spanned fifty-seven acres, and like many of the town's largest estates, it housed a working farm. In addition to the beautiful mansion, with its east side facing the Long Island Sound, offering sailors views of its slate roof and sloping eaves, the property that would come to be known for decades as the Greenway estate was also home to fruit-bearing orchards, chickens, pigs and vegetables planted for consumption. Dogs and horses also called the grounds home.

These amenities helped the estate sustain itself, but it was still a "gentleman's estate," and the hay barn and poultry shed shared the grounds with a tennis court, beach and private moorings where the Greenways could keep their sailboats, which they used to reach the private islands they owned off the coast.

After the original purchase in 1905, the Greenway family continued to add to the estate, tacking on parcels of land until it encompassed more than one hundred acres, with waterside frontage on the Mianus River as well as the Long Island Sound. Gourlie's original house, Kincraig, was expanded as well.

The Greenways added two wings to the building seven years after first purchasing the home, completing the Neo-Renaissance mansion. The estate became recognized throughout town as one of Greenwich's finest, and assessment records show that as the family continued to accumulate land, Kincraig and its grounds became one of the most valuable properties Greenwich had ever seen.

In 1930, the property had the fifth-highest assessed value in Greenwich, at $1.1 million, behind the Condé Nast Publishing Company, Percy Rockefeller's estate, Indian Spring Land Company and Rhea Reid Topping. By 1939, it had risen to the fourth highest, overtaking Percy Rockefeller's estate, which had sold a considerable amount of land over the years.

Like the Rockefellers, the Lauder-Greenway family sold and gave away bits of its land over the years. In fact, the family became just as well known for their generosity in giving pieces of the property away as they had for assembling the coastline compound. In 1918, Harriet and James donated one of their islands to the town of Greenwich to be used for recreation. Great Captains Island, which lies about two miles south of Greenwich Harbor, is now home to one of the town's most popular summertime spots, Island Beach.

Two years after donating the island, the family also donated the first Island Beach ferry to the town of Greenwich, providing transportation for up to two hundred visitors per trip. While the ferry was originally reserved for town residents with limited guest access, the service, which leaves from the landing at Roger Sherman Baldwin Park, was opened up to out-of-towners

The Gilded Age on Connecticut's Gold Coast

in the summer of 2008. Now more than 100,000 visits to the beach are accounted for each year.

In addition to founding Island Beach Park, the Lauder-Greenway property was further split when Harriet gifted a parcel to her daughter and another to a local school. The railroad and Interstate 95, which now run through just north of the existing estate, also gobbled up portions of the property over the years.

After the death of Harriet and James's son Lauder in 1981, the remaining estate was sold out of the family for $7.5 million in a private sale to timber tycoon John Rudey, who continued to own the estate for three decades. In its second life after the Greenways, the property has come to be known as Copper Beech Farm, so named for the majestic trees that provide a canopy over the private seaside escape. Of the total fifty acres still attached to the estate, more than forty are assessed as forestland.

The farm made a big splash in the spring of 2013, when it hit the real estate market with a price tag of $190 million, making it the most expensive listing ever seen on the public market in America. The property itself is now split into two parcels; one is twenty acres and the other just over than thirty. And in addition to the farm, Copper Beech also lays claim to two islands that were included in the listing, bringing the total shoreline frontage up to more than four thousand feet.

The listing, handled by Greenwich's own David Ogilvy & Associates, boasted "amazing views, extraordinary walled gardens, unbelievable privacy, a seventy-five-foot pool with a spa, a beach, a grass tennis court, a superb greenhouse, a stone carriage house and a cottage in a totally convenient and quiet location."

The sprawling twelve-bedroom house, with 13,500 square feet of living space, still bared a great resemblance to the mansion as it had looked when the Greenways called it home, with a paneled library complete with a fireplace, bow window and curved glass bookcases and a master suite with its own fireplace, sleeping porch, dressing room and a marble bathroom. The listing also described five other bedrooms on the main floor: two were oval, with one including a fireplace; one had a fireplace and a sleeping porch; and another two had access to a large balcony. Another four bedrooms were located on the third floor.

As with any great Greenwich mansion, the house also boasted a wine cellar, which was situated near the original staff kitchen on the lower level. The stone-and-shingle façade still appeared as it had in the Gilded Age, with stone turrets flanking the main entrance, 1,800 feet down the winding driveway from the gatehouse. On the shore side, the eaves and pitches still sweep across the house, adding an elegant, old-world touch.

But with all these original details, the house was in need of renovation at the time of the listing. Since the land was situated in a part of town designated with two-acre zoning, subdividing the estate could prove to be a lucrative option, and most of the property's value came from the extensive grounds rather than the home itself.

The first public listing of the property since 1904 drew recognition across the country, both for its price tag (which was reduced by $50 million a few short months after the initial listing, amid reports that the property carried more than $100 million in debt) and for the unique features the property possessed as one of the last great estates of Greenwich.

While many of Greenwich's finest estates were situated along the shores of the Long Island Sound, backcountry Greenwich—the northernmost part of town—has also set itself apart as a destination for the privileged few seeking one-of-a-kind properties.

Chapter 7
A Gentleman's Estate at Conyers Farm

Conyers Farm, an expansive swath of land in the northern portion of Greenwich, with wayward fingers stretching into New York State, is known today as one of the most exclusive gated communities in the entire United States. But back in the early twentieth century, the estate—which, when totaled, includes more land than New York City's Central Park and Brooklyn's Prospect Park combined—was just one man's gentleman's estate.

Edmund Cornelius Converse was a steel industrialist who sat on the executive board of United States Steel Corporation along with John D. Rockefeller, J. Pierpont Morgan, and several other men known to be the most powerful in the nation at that time. In addition to his work in steel, Converse was also a financier. He served as president of the Bankers' Trust Company, beginning at its organization in 1903, and held key positions in other trust companies and banks during his career. In 1918, he was named president of the Greenwich Trust Company.

By that time, Converse was a familiar face in the town of Greenwich. He spent several summers in Belle Haven as a seasonal Greenwich resident. Then, shortly after 1900, Converse began buying up land from several different families in the rural northern portion of Greenwich, cobbling together a large property that grew to more than 1,400 acres at its height. And in 1903, he began constructing buildings on the land, designing a self-sufficient farm reminiscent of an old English manor. At the center of the estate was his mansion, built of stone cut from the quarries on his own property and crowned with a green tile roof, spitting several chimneys into the sky.

The Gilded Age on Connecticut's Gold Coast

E.G. Converse's home at Conyers Manor in backcountry Greenwich was constructed from fieldstones picked from a quarry on the 1,400-acre estate. *Courtesy of the Library of Congress.*

The massive fieldstone building, with fifty-two total rooms, was set on the highest point on the estate and had commanding views that stretched all the way to Long Island Sound on the south and to far corners of the countryside in other directions.

"When you came up the driveway to the entrance, there was a high portecochère. Big doors opened from here into a marble vestibule," Eleanor Marie Enright remembered in an oral history given in 1974.

Enright grew up on nearby North Street and served as secretary to the farm's manager between 1934 and 1950. Her connection to the farm ran deep. Before her, Enright's mother had been secretary to the estate's manager from 1903 to 1910 when the manor was being developed; her aunt held that same position between 1910 and 1918.

"If you've ever seen any of the houses in Newport, well, this was every bit as fine as any of them. In fact, even finer, I think," Enright said.

From the front, the house resembled an old English manor, just as Converse had hoped, with ivy crawling up the sides of the fieldstone façade and gables and dormers adding triangular accents to the roofline. In front of the home was

Transforming Greenwich, Stamford and Darien

A 1908 photo of the interior of E.G. Converse's backcountry home shows an elaborately decorated room with a balcony, paintings, fireplace, grandfather clock and elk head. *Courtesy of the Library of Congress.*

a large lily pond surrounded by well-kept green lawns. From the side, the house took on new depth as wings extended in several different directions, adding more square footage than one would have originally guessed. Porches holding wicker furniture and pergolas, trimmed with dangling greens meandered onto the ground, created a mixture of indoor and outdoor spaces.

Visitors to the mansion were first greeted in a two-story vestibule with white marble floors, a pipe organ and a fireplace. There, a beautiful staircase led upstairs to a hallway lined with paintings hanging on green damask-

The Gilded Age on Connecticut's Gold Coast

The billiard room in E.G. Converse's backcountry Greenwich mansion as photographed in 1908. It is complete with deer and elk heads mounted on the wall. *Courtesy of the Library of Congress.*

covered walls. The hall was laced with balconies, overlooking this dramatic entrance. The main portion of the first floor could entertain hundreds of people comfortably, and knights' armor stood in corners and along walls in this space, creating Converse's desired feel of an old English manor house. But in addition to the massive dining room, library, billiards room, reception area and other main rooms—many of which were paneled in Circassian walnut or mahogany, according to Enright—the Conyers mansion boasted a one-of-a-kind suite for its master.

While Converse kept his main office in New York City, his country workspace had all the exquisite amenities one would expect in Manhattan, with walls covered in beautiful Moroccan leather. In addition to his office, Converse's personal suite included a trophy room with built-in gun cases, which Enright guessed were made from the wood of a pecan tree, adding, "It was beautiful." The suite was also home to an exercise room, a steam bath and a two-lane bowling alley—a true rarity in that time, even for mega

Transforming Greenwich, Stamford and Darien

This photo shows E.G. Converse's study in his backcountry Greenwich home, complete with a portrait of a lady in Elizabethan dress, a buffalo statue, a mounted elk head and a grandfather clock. *Courtesy of the Library of Congress.*

estates like those popping up along the Greenwich countryside. "It was a very fine way for a busy man to keep in shape and also to entertain his business associates," Enright explained.

Converse's bedroom was massive, complete with a marble fireplace and mantel, and his bathroom was equally luxurious—"big enough to have a party," according to Enright—with marble all around and ornate fixtures. "The opulence of those early days was fantastic," Enright said in her interview.

Palatial as parts of the home were, there were also sections that were a bit more down-to-earth and utilitarian. On the west end of the building, for instance, there were servants' quarters, a sewing room, a linen room, a pressing room and other areas equipped for day-to-day duties on the estate.

"In the back of the house there was a walled courtyard, and from that you would go into the kitchen and the downstairs servants' dining room,

The Gilded Age on Connecticut's Gold Coast

This 1908 photograph of Conyers Manor shows the windmill-shaped clock tower at left and a garage at right. *Courtesy of the Library of Congress.*

laundry, and places like that, with all the storage rooms for supplies," Enright said, adding that "you wouldn't see this area from the front of the house at all."

That dichotomy of ornate beauty on one side and pure utility on the other ran through the rest of the estate as well. On the south side of the house, an old English garden graced the grounds, complete with an oblong reflecting pool in the middle. The garden joined a stone terrace that met with the house's main hall, giving guests and residents an easy route to the over-the-top plantings.

In addition to the formal gardens, Conyers Farm also held several greenhouses, where everything from palm trees and nectarines to orchids were grown year round. Many of the outbuildings in these parts of the property were ornate—the manor stables were built from stone, just like the main house—but much of what took place on the grounds served purposes that ran much deeper than luxury and vanity.

The manor house sat near the southeastern corner of the property, where guests first entered the sprawling grounds. But a trip slightly south and west of the main home led to the farm buildings used to keep the estate running. After he purchased property from a large number of families to assemble his estate, Converse kept many of the original houses intact, and they continued to serve roughly two hundred employees as homes. At one time, there were more than forty buildings on the property, many of which were simple edifices constructed to help run the farm, which included acres of hayfields, woodland and an apple orchard.

When Converse died in 1921, most of his estate was willed to his widow and children. But after his passing, the expansive grounds became too much for his family to handle, so in 1927, his widow put the property up for sale.

Transforming Greenwich, Stamford and Darien

A pergola in the home of E.G. Converse in backcountry Greenwich. This photo was taken in 1908. Courtesy of the Library of Congress.

Originally purchased by a man named Frederick Sansome in 1928 for $2 million (roughly $24.7 million in today's dollars), the property was later taken over by the bank when the Great Depression hit the nation and Sansome found himself unable to keep up with the $800,000 mortgage he had taken out on the manor. In the coming years, many of the buildings were torn down, and the property was subdivided several times.

As the decades wore on, it seemed unlikely that a manor such as the one assembled by Converse could ever return to its original grandeur. But in 1980, Greenwich resident Peter Brant purchased more than 1,400 acres of the previous Conyers Manor for $18 million. Like Converse before him, Brant—who was only thirty-two years old at the time—was known around Greenwich as a sort of modern captain of industry. He owned newsprint companies as well as publications like *Interview* and *Art in America*. A highly ranked amateur polo player and horse breeder, Brant lived at White Birch Farm, a 200-acre estate near the former Converse property, and his plans for the manor included turning it into an equestrian's paradise.

The Gilded Age on Connecticut's Gold Coast

During World War II, the farm buildings at Conyers Farm in backcountry Greenwich were neglected. *Photo courtesy of the* Greenwich Time.

While Greenwich zoning laws dictated that lots in the backcountry neighborhood encompass a minimum of four acres, Brant's vision of a community of polo enthusiasts taking up residence in a rural paradise led him to set a minimum lot size at ten acres. In total, Brant created ninety-five separate parcels, where large mansions grew out of even larger lawns. When buyers began purchasing their parcels in 1983, the *New York Times* reported that the estimated price of building a home in the community totaled a minimum of $1.2 million when the land, water and septic, road connection and building were all tallied up.

Three decades after Brant set his dream into motion, Conyers Farm has come to be known as one of the most majestic communities for America's wealthiest families in all of the Northeast, boasting everything from celebrity residents—including Academy Award–winning director Ron Howard and actors like Mel Gibson, to name a few—to the world-class polo pitch, which has played host to some of the best players alive. In 2013 alone, the Greenwich Polo Club enjoyed visits from Prince Harry, who traveled to America to play a charity match on the field, as well as Facundo Pieres, the world's highest-ranked polo player.

Transforming Greenwich, Stamford and Darien

These days, Greenwich is known as the "hedge fund capital of the world," cementing Greenwich's legacy as a place where money is made, traded and spent on tremendous estates like the ones found in the town's backcountry and down on the shore.

And while the perfectly maintained stone walls and lush lawns of communities like Conyers Farm, Belle Haven and other beautiful neighborhoods in Greenwich give the impression that the area has been a first-class hideout for the rich and famous since the world began, the truth is that it's simply the lasting impression left on southwestern Fairfield County by captains of industry who transformed this once rural landscape into a swath of country estates, creating a community unlike any other in the nation.

Chapter 8

STAMFORD SEES CHANGES OF ITS OWN

Directly bordering Greenwich on its east side is the city of Stamford. With industrial roots and a current population of more than 120,000 people (roughly twice as many residents as Greenwich claims), making it the third-largest city in Connecticut, Stamford is significantly different from its western neighbor in many ways. But in the late 1800s, the two communities experienced a very similar tug in their fabrics. As captains of industry set their sights on Greenwich, other wealthy Americans focused on Stamford. Some of these new Stamford residents brought innovation, while others brought dreams of quiet times, relaxing along the city's rocky shores.

The city of Stamford went through a pronounced and dramatic period of change in the years around the turn of the twentieth century.

In 1912, to mark the twentieth anniversary of continuous daily printing of the city's newspaper, the *Daily Advocate* devoted thousands of words to examining the two decades since it had switched from weekly to daily publication on April 4, 1892. Looking back, the *Advocate* wrote that it was "recalled that people were referring then to the decade between 1880 and 1890 as the most progressive in the town's history. There were optimizing people in Stamford in 1892, and yet few, if any, among its prophets would have felt encouraged to predict the material progress which was to take place in the next two decades. To describe that now, or even to summarize it, would require many pages of a publication like this."

The anniversary edition went on to explore the city's growth in a variety of measures, noting that the twenty-year span saw the doubling of Stamford's population, which went from sixteen thousand people to thirty-

The Gilded Age on Connecticut's Gold Coast

A view of Columbus Park in downtown Stamford at the turn of the twentieth century. *Courtesy of the* Stamford Advocate.

Stamford's historic post office as photographed in 1916. The building, which is listed on the National Register of Historic Places, ceased operation as a post office in the fall of 2013. *Courtesy of the Library of Congress.*

two thousand people. "But the census tells only a small part of the story of twenty years," the *Advocate* declared. "Its wealth, estimated at real-estate values, has considerably more than doubled. The grand list of the town was $9,000,000. Today it is $37,000,000."

Transforming Greenwich, Stamford and Darien

The entrance to Stamford's Town Hall stood on Bank Street during the period when this photo was taken in the early 1880s. *Courtesy of the Stamford Advocate.*

That time period also saw the official certification of Stamford as a city, after having been recognized as a borough for many years. And its new status was accompanied by a significant number of additions to the city's offerings. Between 1892 and 1912, Stamford Hospital was built, as well as a new town hall and new buildings for the city's YMCA and Ferguson Library. Three fire stations and "modern equipment" for the paid firefighting force were also initiated. More than one thousand homes were added to the city's ranks, transforming pastures and farmland into residential neighborhoods and spurring the establishment of dozens of new roads and streets. While the city's first complete directory, published in 1883, catalogued 130 streets throughout Stamford, the steady growth and expansion of the city's residential life added roughly 300 more in the next thirty years.

To accommodate the booming population, the city built new schools. According to the *Advocate*, the average attendance grew from 1,606 students in 1891 to 2,728 in 1901 and 4,236 in 1911, a growth of more than 250 percent. By 1916, there were a total of thirty-one schools in the city, up from seventeen in 1891.

While new school buildings were opened and expanded across the city (in fact, the school at Henry Street was the only one that did not require an addition in that stretch of time), perhaps the most significant in that time was the new high school building, which required several additions during

The Gilded Age on Connecticut's Gold Coast

the period as the enrollment swelled beyond people's belief. In 1891, a four-room high school existed on Franklin Street, in the city's downtown area, but by 1912, the building had room for three hundred students.

The railroad stretch between New York City and Stamford was electrified, a new railroad station was erected and a trolley service began, providing easy access to the city's hot spots, like Shippan Point.

As the city stretched to reach new heights, the wealth of its residents also increased. It was noted not only by the quadrupling of the city's grand list

In this undated sketch by Stamford artist Whitman Bailey, people are seen milling around the front of People's Nation Bank of Stamford, which stood at 433 Main Street, where the ramp to the city's mall, Stamford Town Center, now stands. *Courtesy of the Stamford Advocate.*

but also through deposit amounts in Stamford's banks. In 1892, when there were four banking institutions in town, a total of $5.3 million in deposits was recorded, according to the *Advocate*. Twenty years later, another bank had joined Stamford's ranks—the Fidelity Title and Trust Company—and the deposit total had ballooned to $14.4 million. "And, better than all, a public spirit which finds expression in a confident outlook for Stamford's future," the newspaper wrote.

But even as Stamford grew rapidly, the turn of the twentieth century still saw a city with rural touches, according to the *Advocate*: "The outskirts of the city, in each direction, is a charming rolling country, with good roads and delightful drives, the various landscapes dotted here and there with homes of ancient and modern architecture, fine lawns, and well-kept grounds that are made doubly attractive by their rural environment."

This existed in harmony with a central boom. As the *Advocate* wrote in 1912, Stamford was "bounding into greater prominence and desirability every year, it is too attractive and too conveniently situated to remain standing still."

New neighborhoods were forming all the time. The twentieth anniversary edition of the *Daily Advocate* described several such communities that had risen to prominence in recent years, including Springdale, Courtland Terrace and Southfield Point, down in the shore area near Shippan.

The newspaper also described a new development called Revonah Manor in great detail:

> *The recent inland development is a delightful community that offers superior inducements to those who are seeking a location of the best type. It is situated in the finest residential section, within the limits of the city, has splendid macadam roads, concrete walks, brick gutters, and is fully equipped with sewer, city water, gas and electric lights. The drainage is perfect. The grounds are rolling and picturesque, the air is healthful, the neighborhood is one of refinement, and everything is here that will make life worth living. It is an ideal location of those who delight in rural comfort yet do not care to be deprived of the convenience of the city.*

An ad for the community—billed as a "high-class restricted development in the finest residential section of Stamford"—also published in 1912, touted Revonah Manor's proximity to New York City at roughly an hour's commute. It boasted, "Every requirement is here for a desirable suburban home. Clean and attractive streets lead from the railway station to the property," adding

The Gilded Age on Connecticut's Gold Coast

The grotto at Shippan Point served as a place for cows to graze in the early 1900s. This photo was taken for a circa 1911 postcard. *Courtesy of the* Stamford Advocate.

that "Revonah Manor is conveniently situated. It is within the city limits, the trolley car only a short distance away, and it is but ten minutes to the railway station."

An assortment of advertisements from old editions of Stamford's newspaper paint a picture of a city that marketed itself as a place that offered something for everyone—a home for those seeking a country or a city life.

The official souvenir program for the city's 275th anniversary, published in 1916, proclaimed that "Stamford's area of thirty-eight square miles offers the ideal combination of sea shore, hills and dales; picturesque grouping of gray granite boulders and dark foliaged cedars, rivulets cascading joyously over stone ledges on their way back to the sea; peaceful pasture lands gently sloping to the shore; pictures at every vista, pictures which have lured noted artists from the city studios."

The program went on to describe the "five miles of alluring water frontage, whose imposing bluffs are bulkheaded by Nature, and indented with coves and inlets, making safe little harbors for moorings, with sunny beaches for happy children."

Much of this water frontage, which proved to be among the top attractors for summer residents, was located in Shippan, a peninsula in the southernmost part of the city that transformed from a span of open land with grazing cows and green pastures into a residential neighborhood of beautiful homes that remains the most coveted corner of Stamford today.

Chapter 9
STAMFORD'S SHIPPAN DEVELOPS INTO A SEASIDE RESORT

Nearly four hundred years after Stamford was first settled, there is still a mystery surrounding how the peninsula of Shippan received its name. Local legend circulating through the city in the nineteenth century claimed that the "Ship Anne," named for England's Queen Anne, found itself shipwrecked at the peninsula during the queen's reign. But the original deed that procured the land the city sits upon from local Native Americans mentioned Wascusee as the "Sagamore of Shippan" more than two decades before the queen was born.

Regardless of where the name springs from, Shippan has gained a national reputation as a prized seaside community, complete with salty air, lapping waves and wide water views. In fact, Shippan's beauty has been a poorly kept secret for more than two hundred years.

Norwalk native Moses Rogers, who made a fortune for himself in New York City and was at one point a director of the United States Bank, was one of the first outsiders to use the rocky point on Stamford's most southern tip as a wealthy man's playground. He acquired a large estate over several years, beginning in 1799, when he paid $8,000 for a little more than one hundred acres of land. He added another seventy-four acres to his holdings the following year, and in 1806, he bought a two-hundred-acre estate for $10,000, giving him ownership to roughly a quarter of the entire area. A few years later, he erected a mansion on the east side of Shippan Avenue, near what is now Ocean Drive East, and began welcoming guests, many of whom were awestruck by the splendor of Shippan.

The Gilded Age on Connecticut's Gold Coast

Whitman Bailey's 1933 sketch of Shippan's Cummings Park. *Courtesy of the* Stamford Advocate.

In 1812, Roger's brother-in-law Timothy Dwight, who was a former president of Yale College, described a visit to Shippan in his book, *Travels in New England*. "The surface slopes in every direction, and is encircled by a collection of exquisite scenery," he wrote of the rock-laced point. "The Sound and Long Island beyond it, with a gracefully indented shore, are directly in front, and both stretch westward to a vast distance and eastward until the eye is lost."

The peninsula captured his heart—not only because of the water views but also the farm's orchards and groves tucked away from the water. "Here Mr. Rogers has formed an avenue, a mile in length, reaching quite to the water's edge. At the same time, he has united plantations of fruit trees, a rich garden, and other interesting objects, so combined as to make this one of the pleasantest retreats in the United States."

Rogers enjoyed his estate for several years before passing away in 1825, at which point he willed the land to members of his family, which included two sons, a daughter, several grandchildren and his brothers and nephews. The mansion house, along with eighteen acres and several of the estate's outbuildings, were rented by Isaac Bragg for $400 a year very shortly after

Rogers's death. Bragg ran a boys' boarding school on the property for several years, but a lack of oversight and upkeep allowed the estate to fall into disrepair. It was not restored to its previous glory until 1845, when a new tenant, S.E. Lawrence, moved in.

But when Rogers's youngest child, Sarah Elizabeth Hopkins, died in upstate New York in 1866, the land's future became much less certain. For the next several years, parts of the parcel were sold off in public auction, and the large estate was dismantled piece by piece. This marked a turning point in Shippan's history, as smaller plots sprinkled throughout the peninsula meant that more individual families could stake a claim on the land, creating the basis for a popular residential neighborhood.

In March 1867, for example, a ten-acre parcel of land near the middle of the peninsula was sold to Sally Scofield for $980. An advertisement in *Harper's Weekly*, published on October 9, 1869, describes some of the land up for sale on the block, writing that Shippan "is a beautiful and fertile peninsula of 300 acres in extent opposite Stamford, Connecticut. The surface slopes in every direction, and it is surrounded on all sides by the most exquisite scenery. In front, stretching westward and seaward for a long distance, lies Long Island Sound, with Long Island beyond. Through the groves and orchards of Shippan Point several miles of serpentine roads have been recently constructed, and other improvements are in progress."

By the 1870s, the area was subdivided into four hundred one-acre estates, prime for single-family residences. New roads sprung up along the boundaries, including Verplank Avenue, which runs east–west off of Shippan Avenue near the tip, and Van Rensselaer Avenue, which runs perpendicular to Verplank. Both streets were named after Rogers's heirs. It was another four decades until Rogers Road, on the west side of the point, was named for Moses Rogers.

"It is not surprising that Stamford has long attracted wide attention as a summer resort, and every year entertains a large and increasing number of temporary residents," read an entry in Stamford's 1879–80 directory. The entry continued, boasting Stamford's proximity to New York City, which made its location "more convenient or more accessible for a business man whose family, for health's sake must spend the summer in the country, but who, himself, cannot wholly leave his affairs in other hands."

At that time, the directory pointed out that more than one hundred commuters traveled daily between Stamford and New York City in both the winter and the summer, further noting that "in the last named season, this number more than doubles."

The Gilded Age on Connecticut's Gold Coast

This 1906 postcard asks the question of which cottage should be rented for the summer season. *Courtesy of the* Stamford Advocate.

And as Stamford's fame grew, the small neighborhood of Shippan became even more desired among elite families in the greater New York area. In the official souvenir program of Stamford's 275th anniversary, inked in 1916, it is noted that Shippan was originally developed "as an exclusive summer residential section, the little colony consisting largely of New York people who appreciated the advantages sufficiently to build costly mansions of architectural beauty."

And scores of New York City's well-to-do families flooded the peninsula's properties for summer stays over the years. An article published in the *New York Times* in July 1894 lists more than forty couples and families who took leave of Manhattan for the shores of Shippan that season. "The nearness of this seaside resort to New York makes it a favorite with many people from the metropolis," the report states. "It can be reached in less than an hour from the Grand Central Station, being only a mile or two from Stamford."

One of the best-known residences on the point is Marion Castle, the Neo-Renaissance palace built in 1913 for silent film magnate Frank J. Marion. The seven-story castle was designed by the Manhattan-based architectural firm of Hunt & Hunt, which rose to prominence during the Gilded Age as the preferred firm of America's most powerful men. In addition to designing ornate, high-profile houses in Newport, Rhode Island, and Tuxedo Park, New York, Hunt & Hunt was also responsible for the "Marble Twins"—two Beaux-Arts-style mansions the firm created for George W. Vanderbilt at 645 and 647 Fifth Avenue in New York City. While 645 was later torn down, 647

Transforming Greenwich, Stamford and Darien

Marion Castle, at 1 Rogers Road, was the palatial home of silent-film mogul Frank J. Marion in the 1910s. *Courtesy of the* Stamford Advocate.

was designated a New York City landmark and still stands, now serving as the location for Versace's flagship store.

But perhaps the most high-profile creations completed by Hunt & Hunt occurred at another one of Vanderbilt's properties; the firm designed his Asheville, North Carolina mansion, the Biltmore, which remains America's largest home, with more than four acres of living space inside, including thirty-five bedrooms, forty-three bathrooms and more than five dozen fireplaces.

In Shippan, the white stucco house topped with a slate roof was situated on a long, narrow strip of land that slopes downward on the west side as Shippan's shoreline descends into the Sound's waters. In a 1916 edition of the *Architectural Record*, a writer notes that this topographical challenge forced the architects to build the chateau on the property's crest, further from the water than many other homes. This "enabled the architects to develop a beautiful terrace garden commanding a magnificent view of the Sound," according to the magazine, which includes a romantic description of the mansion, declaring that "the house recalls the French chateau and, like its prototype, its entrance door, to the east, gives directly upon the sidewalk, the gentle curve of the street being echoed in the contour of the house."

Inside, great open fireplaces, inviting lounges and a pipe organ created a warm environment in which the Marion family could relax. Like many

The Gilded Age on Connecticut's Gold Coast

turn-of-the-century homes, a grand staircase greeted guests just past the main entrance, sweeping one's eyes to the high ceilings and grand features of one of Shippan's most extravagant homes.

"In the northern end of the house is a library, and beyond it is a typical French tower, which, however, besides its circular stairway, contains that very modern feature, an elevator," the magazine writes.

The home cost $140,000 to construct, which translates to roughly $3.3 million in today's dollars. And the architects thought of everything. In a 1967 interview with the *New York Times*, the owners who had purchased the castle after Marion's death four years before noted that it is totally fortified, including "everything but the moat." According to Martha Cogan, who owned the house along with her husband, David, they "could be besieged and withstand an attack." With thirty-two-inch-thick walls, built of brick over reinforced concrete and steel beams, the home could certainly serve as a fort should Shippan ever need one.

In an undated real estate flyer for the property on file at the Stamford Historical Society, the castle is marketed as having "an atmosphere of splendor within its marble halls and staircases," noting that while the massive home (with at least seven bedrooms, plus four more for maids) has plenty of floor space, portions could easily be closed off to make housekeeping easier.

"Set on five beautiful landscaped acres of formal gardens, orchards, perennials, spring bulbs and lovely lawns which sweep toward the water and sand swimming beach; this exceptional property is screened by ancient, knarled [*sic*] shade trees and fine boxwood for complete privacy," the real estate brochure details, adding that "from the waterfront, with its barbecue area and dock, a panoramic view of Stamford Harbor unfolds including the harbor breakwater and beyond to Long Island Sound. On clear days, the New York skyline is visible twenty-seven miles away."

The home was later named to the National Register of Historic Places in 1982, and it is the only building in Shippan to earn that distinction. But its owners have cared deeply about the preservation of Shippan since the castle's inception. One lamp in the castle is decorated with an inscription, written on parchment, that reads, "Pre ser veth econt i nui tyof oce and rivew est." It might look like an ancient motto, torn from the pages of a Latin or Greek tale, but in fact, it's an English phrase with the spaces between the words rearranged. It means, "Preserve the continuity of Ocean Drive West."

Even now, in the twenty-first century, the home remains one of Stamford's most interesting residences. But the original family who lived at the castle was just as fascinating. Frank J. Marion was known as a groundbreaking filmmaker and pioneer who sometimes found himself embroiled in controversy. As a frontrunner in silent films, Marion's first blockbuster was a fifteen-minute version of *Ben Hur*, which he produced in 1907. The film contained sixteen scenes and fit on one reel of film—as most of Marion's movies did—but Marion's version did not earn its acclaim for the same reasons as later movie versions of the story.

After the movie was distributed, Henry Wallace—son of *Ben Hur* author Lew Wallace, who had first published the book a quarter of a century earlier—sued Marion's production company, Kalem Company, for copyright infringement. In 1910, a U.S. Supreme Court order ruled that Kalem Company did in fact infringe on the author's rights, mandating that Marion pay Wallace's heirs $25,000 and setting a precedent for the need for filmmakers to obtain rights from a book's author before producing another version.

In the coming years, Kalem also became the first U.S. film company to shoot a movie on location overseas when Marion sent a crew to Beaufort, Ireland, in 1910 to film *A Lad from Old Ireland*.

While Marion came to be known as one of the most famous filmmakers of the silent film era—often referred to as "the king of one-reel films"—he wasn't Stamford's only celebrity known for bringing stories to life for audiences. John Lester Wallack was one of America's most famous actors in the latter portion of the nineteenth century. In an obituary that ran after his death in the late summer of 1888, the *New York Times* declared that "Lester Wallack, with the single exception of Edwin Booth, was the best-known American actor of his time."

Born in New York City, Wallack studied acting in Great Britain before returning to the States in the 1847–48 theater season for his first American role as Sir Charles Coldstream in *Used Up* at the Broadway Theater. He was prolific in the coming years, bringing dozens of characters to life in a very real way, thanks to his diligence in character study.

"In all the time of his service in this country, he had few rivals in polite comedy and the romantic drama. In his youth, he was everybody's beau ideal of the stage lover," the *Times* wrote in the obituary, adding that "his list of characters was not only long, but surprisingly varied."

Several years later, in 1861, Wallack opened the Star Theater at Broadway and Thirteenth Street. It was New York City's first comedy theater and came to be known as one of the city's top venues.

While he spent a considerable amount of time in New York City, Wallack also kept a home just outside the Shippan neighborhood, near the Cove section of Stamford, on the grounds of what is now a gated community

The Gilded Age on Connecticut's Gold Coast

bearing his name: Wallacks Point. His estate there, which he dubbed Elmsmere, served primarily as a summer residence for his family for just shy of a dozen years.

At the time of his death, it was reported that while he did not have many public associations with the city's residents, he was acquainted with and held in high regard by a good number of Stamford's citizens. And his property was one of the finest in town.

A few days after the obituary, the *Times* ran a second story chronicling Wallack's well-attended funeral and describing his beautiful country estate:

> *Two miles and a half to the eastward of Stamford lies Elmsmere, the Summer home of the Wallacks, its broad acres of wood and greensward stretching away till they terminate in seawall and beach, washed by the waters of Long Island Sound. A short distance off shore are the rocks that beat in the hull of the Bridgeport steamer* Idlewild *nearly three years ago. The driveway that leads through the estate is a continuation of Sound View Avenue which ends abruptly at the large stone gateway. Back from the driveway stands the house, overlooking closely clipped lawns and the sea. No sail is visible; nothing but fog, trees, patches of dark red show through the heavy foliage.*

The star-studded legacy of Shippan and other areas by the shore in Stamford doesn't end with Wallack and Marion. Celebrities have continued to call the area home through modern day. In 1979, Faye Dunaway paid $775,000—roughly $2.5 million today—for a fifteen-room Mediterranean-style mansion on three acres of waterfront property.

Today, Wallacks Drive extends all the way down to the Long Island Sound, where a set of wrought-iron gates—moved to Stamford from in front of the Star Theater by Wallack himself in the late 1800s—ensure privacy. Behind the gates lies a man-made access road that connects the mainland with the three-and-a-half-acre Caritas Island, upon which sits the three-story mansion constructed shortly after the turn of the century for James Graham Phelps Stokes, majestically overlooking the peaceful waters just as it has for more than one hundred years.

Stokes was the son of Anson Phelps Stokes, who claimed a summer house in Darien, as well as the younger brother of Isaac Newton Phelps Stokes, who designed and lived in Greenwich's High-Low House. While born to a powerful and wealthy family, "Graham," as he was known, was an outspoken advocate for social reforms. In 1902, at the age of thirty, he moved away

Transforming Greenwich, Stamford and Darien

The secluded Caritas Island has been a well-hidden Stamford gem for decades. *Courtesy of the* Stamford Advocate.

from his lavish family home and took up residence in a settlement house on Manhattan's poor Lower East Side to become a social worker. It was about that time that he met Rose Pastor, a reporter for the *Jewish Daily News*, who interviewed him for a story she penned that praised him for his ideals. The pair fell in love, and on July 18, 1905, they were married at his parents' summer house in Darien.

The couple joined the Socialist Party of America and in 1905 helped found the Intercollegiate Socialist Society, along with men such as Upton Sinclair and Jack London. That same year, Stokes ran for public office for the first time, unsuccessfully vying for the role of president on the New York Board of Aldermen; his name was second on a ticket that was headlined by mayoral candidate William Randolph Hearst.

In 1909, Stokes's home on Caritas Island, which was named for the Latin word for "charity," was constructed. The twenty-four-thousand-square-foot stone mansion has eleven bedrooms, ten and a half bathrooms and four fireplaces.

The Stokes family owned the property for several years, at one time renting the island to *Collier's Weekly* managing editor John O'Hara Cosgrave in 1916. The island and the home have changed hands several times over the course of the decades. In April 1950, Benjamin D. Gilbert and his wife, Mary Adeline Prentice Gilbert, a granddaughter of John D. Rockefeller, purchased the property from Harris Weissbuch. It was later bought by J.P. Morgan's great-great-grandson John Adams Morgan (who is also a descendant of the American president John Adams) in 1987.

The Gilded Age on Connecticut's Gold Coast

James S. Herrman's estate on Ocean Drive East was one of the larger homes in Shippan. *Courtesy of the* Stamford Advocate.

The Shippan Point Hotel provided a place to stay for summer visitors during the years when Shippan became en vogue. *Courtesy of the* Stamford Advocate.

Not every Shippan resident came from a family with an unforgettable surname. One of the most breathtaking homes to grace the shoreline was constructed for New York builder James Herrmann just after 1900. His massive home sat on seven acres of shorefront property.

A July 1958 article in the *Stamford Shopper and Weekly Mail* declared that "Shippan, by its very geography, is perfectly suited to recreational purposes," further noting that "throughout its history, Shippan has remained an area where people live and play, doing their serious work elsewhere."

Transforming Greenwich, Stamford and Darien

With the influx of people coming to Stamford's shore-side community during the summer months, there was a demand for an increase in services and amenities. And Shippan delivered. In July 1894, Stamford resident John McDevitt announced plans to erect a three-story hotel on the point, near the trolley terminus. The hotel, which contained a total of sixteen guest rooms, took less than a year to build and was open for business by the beginning of the next summer season.

In a May 27, 1895 *Stamford Advocate* article, the newspaper described the formal opening of the lodge, which McDevitt named the Waverley Hotel: "The building, both inside and out, was much admired by the visitors, and many expressed themselves that it was but the beginning of a big boom for Shippan Point."

That boom gained momentum over the course of the next few years. In 1896, the Shippan Land Association took significant steps toward creating a "pleasure resort" in the community, complete with "an iron pier 500 feet long, to be used as a landing place for excursion steamers; a half-mile trotting track, and a quarter-mile bicycle track, with suitable place for spectators; large bathing pavilion, and other buildings, including a fine hotel," according to an article published that July in the *Advocate*.

McDevitt's hotel offered a wealth of entertainment options for visitors, with a merry-go-round and a dancing pavilion, which he announced plans

Though the shores of Shippan Point have always been rocky, the salty air and lapping waves have helped make the peninsula a sought-after spot for centuries. *Courtesy of the* Stamford Advocate.

The Gilded Age on Connecticut's Gold Coast

to erect just one year after the hotel first opened. But his Waverley Hotel and all its attractions was not the only option for visitors. There was also the Shippan Point House, purchased by W.B. Buckley in 1896. Under his ownership, the inn grew to become "more enjoyable than ever for its resident guests, and at the same time bring it more in touch with popular appreciation by establishing a café where bathers and other occasional visitors will find refreshment and every attention," according to a June 1896 article in the *Advocate*.

The casino at Shippan Point also made a big splash that same summer, serving as a place where "light theatricals and vaudeville may be enjoyed by the people each evening at popular prices," according to another *Advocate*

While many of the homes that popped up in Shippan during the latter half of the nineteenth century belonged to out-of-towners just beginning to discover the wonders of Stamford, several local families also enjoyed the peninsulas shores. This photo shows the Shippan home of the Gillespies, the Stamford family who owned the city's newspaper. *Courtesy of the* Stamford Advocate.

article published that season.

Summers were a sacred time in Shippan, but Stamford's waterfront neighborhoods didn't remain a summer enclave for New Yorkers for long. Some of Stamford's own wealthy families, including the Gillespies, who owned the *Advocate*, took notice of Shippan's splendors. "Stamford people themselves have become so in love with this beautiful spot that to-day Shippan is one of the choicest of all-year residential sections in this part of the country, offering every advantage that modern complex living demands for its comfort," the *New York Times* wrote.

In an account of life growing up in Shippan between 1910 and 1937, the late Philip Kleinert of Darien described his father's daily commute to New York City. "A good neighbor picked up nearby commuters in his car, drove them to the train in the morning and brought them back at night," he wrote in 1991. "Fortunately, they all seemed to use the same trains."

But carpooling and trains weren't the only option for New York City commuters living down by the sea in Stamford. In 1892, the Stamford Street Railway began a trolley service, connecting the point with the rest of the city—and the cars were pretty regular. On June 7, 1893, the *Advocate* reported that cars would begin their regular run to Shippan for the summer season, with likely service increases as the demand grew. "In a few weeks more, frequent afternoon and evening trips will probably be added," the article stated. "After two additional turnouts have been put in place, should

The steamer *Shadyside* served the Shippan peninsula from 1883 through 1914. *Courtesy of the Stamford Advocate.*

The Gilded Age on Connecticut's Gold Coast

A historic photo of the Ponus Yacht Club on Stamford's South End. *Courtesy of the Stamford Advocate.*

the traffic demand, cars will leave Town Hall every twenty minutes during afternoons, until which hourly trips only will run."

Visitors also came by boat. While some residents may have lined up personal boating options, the use of steamers as a mass transportation option to Shippan sprung up in the 1880s and proved popular.

"Up to the beginning of the Summer of 1886, the arrival and departure of a single daily steamer and the occasional visits of freight propellers or tug boats with lumber or coal-laden barges were the only signs of this marine activity to be seen in our harbor," the 1887–88 Stamford Directory declared. "Since then, a whole fleet of small steam vessels have made their appearance in Stamford waters, chiefly engaged in the business of transporting passengers to and from Shippan point…Besides these, large excursion steamers and barges arrive almost daily at Doerr's from New York."

Boating was an integral part of life in the seaside community during the nineteenth century, and it wasn't long before Shippan residents organized the Stamford Yacht Club. The club opened in 1890 and built its first clubhouse on four acres of land on Shippan Point's west shore, along with bathhouses, horse sheds and more than one hundred feet of dock.

There were several men who came together to organize the club, which became the center of social life on the point, but perhaps none was as important to the cause as Commodore James D. Smith. Smith, who at one point had served as commodore of the New York Yacht Club, came with knowledge for running the operation, as well as ideas gleaned from the posh surroundings in the city club.

Smith was the head of the brokerage house James D. Smith & Co., located on Broadway, and kept a home called Linden Lodge in Stamford. He was a former president of the New York Stock Exchange and continued working on Wall Street until about two weeks before his death at the age of seventy-nine in 1909. In his obituary, the *New York Times* wrote, "For years, James D. Smith was one of the most prominent men in financial, society and yachting circles of this city. Not until the beginning of his fatal illness two weeks ago did he relinquish the control of his affairs in Wall Street."

In addition to being one of the founding fathers of Stamford's club, Smith also served as commodore in 1895–96 and again in 1902–03. His sloop yacht *Pocahontas* was one of the more famous vessels at the clubhouse in the late nineteenth century, and it graced the water alongside other boats with names like *Eclipse* and *Sylph*.

In a tercentenary review of the city of Stamford, published in 1941, the *Stamford Advocate* described the original clubhouse, which formally opened on July 25, 1891, as "a simple, unpretentious structure which soon became the headquarters of a distinguished fraternity of gentlemen."

But an infamous fire in the winter of 1913 destroyed the building, as well as many precious documents pertaining to the club. A year after the fire, the new home of the organization—a sprawling English-style manor house, which today contains more than thirty-six thousand square feet of space—was constructed. These days, the clubhouse is still a hot spot for neighborhood families who flock to the club's pools, tennis and paddle courts and boating programs.

Chapter 10
THE INDUSTRIAL REVOLUTION ACCELERATES GROWTH IN STAMFORD

While Stamford was gaining popularity as a fashionable summer escape for the wealthy in the late 1800s, the city was also growing into a year-round industrial center.

Stamford's identity during the late 1800s was largely influenced by an increase in manufacturing jobs brought to the area during the nation's industrial revolution. The 1879–80 edition of Stamford's directory described this shift, writing that "up to a comparatively recent period, Stamford was not distinctively known as a manufacturing town, but within the last few years, the element of growth and prosperity has received large and significant accessions, and the outlook is that the town is entering upon an era of unprecedented manufacturing progress." And much of that growth was due to one business coming to town: the lock factory of Henry R. Towne and Linus Yale Jr.

"The Yale & Towne Manufacturing Co. is the most important of our industrial institutions," the directory claims. "Its history is a record of that unprecedented expansion and development of the manufacturing interests of Stamford which the last ten years have witnessed, and its growth has been something unique in the history of manufacturing enterprises in this or any other state."

When the Yale Lock Company established itself in Stamford in 1869, with thirty employees, it paved a pathway for monumental growth in the city over the next several decades. By 1872, the number of employees had multiplied by a factor of five—but the company's rise didn't end there. Two decades later, the number was up to about one thousand men and women, accounting for one in every sixteen residents of the budding city.

This rapid, exponential growth was due mostly to a man named Henry R. Towne, an engineer who had learned the trade at the University of Pennsylvania (a college to which his wealthy father, who was an engineer himself, had left $400,000, providing the funds for the Towne Scientific School). Henry R. Towne left school during the Civil War, during which time he worked on the famed battleship *Monitor*. But after peace was declared, he traveled abroad to finish his education in Germany and France.

Shortly after returning to America in the late 1860s, a friend introduced Towne to a Massachusetts man named Linus Yale Jr., an artist and engineer with a deep interest in bank locks. Over the course of many years, Yale had patented several locks, including a new pin-tumbler lock, which opened with a slim, flat key, much unlike the bulky keys in use during that time. While old locks were considered easy to pick, Yale's version (which improved upon an earlier ideas of his father's) featured a lock with several pins of varying lengths that moved in sequence after being triggered by the correct key.

It was clear to Towne that the Yale Lock had serious potential, and if it was to be mass-produced, it could become a true essential for businesses and private citizens the world over. It was this possibility that caught Towne's attention and gave him the idea to pair up with Yale so they could mass-produce the keys. But Towne wasn't the only half of the pair with incredible business skills.

Before ever meeting Towne, Yale had learned to market his locks by exploiting the weaknesses of other locks and ensuring that his products were without these defects. For instance, when promoting the "Yale Magic Infallible Bank Lock," which he created for safes and vaults in 1851, Yale noted nine ways in which it differed from other locks on the market and how these differences made his locks superior. Some of these superiorities included the fact that the intricate sequence of levers and pins that needed to be activated inside his lock to open it meant that it could not be blasted open with gunpowder like many other locks; similarly, its lack of internal springs meant it could not be rendered useless by spring failure as a result of fire or neglect.

In addition, he performed demonstrations for bankers in which he picked locks created by rival companies such as Hobbs—the most prominent bank lock of the day. After his presentations, during which he successfully defeated the Hobbs lock, bankers realized the faults of their current locks and gave Yale a chance.

Transforming Greenwich, Stamford and Darien

Yale and Towne joined forces in 1868 and decided to move the company's headquarters from Yale's native Massachusetts to Stamford, where they could have easy access to the railroad and shipping ports. Yale died unexpectedly that Christmas, after a heart attack, and following the settlement of Yale's estate, Towne came to be the sole owner of the company, which he later renamed Yale & Towne Manufacturing Co.

In a short time, the pin-tumbler lock, which was commonly known as a cylinder lock, lived up to the potential originally imagined by Towne. Door keys, vault keys and safe keys all across the country carried the Yale name on them, thanks to Towne's strict demands for tight copyright control, which helped the company achieve a monopoly. Before long, Stamford had earned a reputation as the "Lock City."

Towne built his new factory in Stamford's South End in 1869 and expanded its grounds in 1883. And his influence in the city grew in a parallel fashion. While he was known as a tough boss, he was also recognized for paying his workers generously and providing them with several benefits, which were spelled out by the *Advocate* in a 1991 article that reviewed the city's industrial past. "He developed his own forward-looking policies that are still models today," the *Advocate* wrote of Towne. "For example, he established a plant hospital; initiated group health and accident insurance, life insurance and retirement pensions; provided a library and offered home building loans, stock purchase plans and anniversary promotions for his employees."

And as his workforce grew, so too did Stamford's fortunes. In a 1941 edition of the *Advocate*, the newspaper declared that the company was "most

Yale & Towne was a groundbreaking company that reached global prominence—all from its headquarters in Stamford, Connecticut. *Courtesy of the* Stamford Advocate.

The Gilded Age on Connecticut's Gold Coast

Piano maker Schleicher & Sons was just one of several industrial businesses based in Stamford during the Gilded Age. *Courtesy of the* Stamford Advocate.

Blickensderfer typewriters also called Stamford home. *Courtesy of the* Stamford Advocate.

Transforming Greenwich, Stamford and Darien

The Stollwerck chocolate company had a home base in Stamford during the Industrial Era. *Courtesy of the* Stamford Advocate.

closely identified with the name and fame of Stamford of all the community's industries," adding that "the story of the growth of this industry in only seventy-three years, from a manufacturing establishment employing only thirty persons to a gigantic enterprise with ramifications throughout the world, follows the best lines of American tradition."

With Towne's employees taking home steady paychecks, the city's men and workingwomen began elevating themselves toward the middle class. In the twenty-five years between 1868, when Towne first arrived in Stamford, and 1893, when he moved his personal residence from an Atlantic Street mansion down to New York City, two commercial banks and a savings bank opened their doors—likely guarded with Yale locks—in town as a result of the economic boom. Yale & Towne's employment figures peaked at five thousand workers in Stamford in 1916.

But the South End factory—which is now home to luxury artist lofts in Stamford's growing Harbor Point neighborhood—was just one of many name brands that came to call Stamford home during this era. The Blickensderfer Typewriter Co., Lincruster-Walton Wallpaper, Schleicher & Sons Piano Co. and the Stollwerck chocolate company also had plants in Stamford, providing jobs for the city's men and women. These companies helped push Stamford further forward from its roots as a rural town, positioning it as a great industrial center by the turn of the century.

The Gilded Age on Connecticut's Gold Coast

While the industrial revolution spurred many changes in Stamford, Darien's transition in this time hinged largely on real estate development—a shift that helped Stamford's small, quiet neighbor retain its peaceful charm while growing rapidly.

Chapter 11
DARIEN'S LONG NECK POINT COMES INTO ITS OWN

Darien's Long Neck Point, like Shippan in Stamford, is a long peninsula that stretches far into Long Island Sound, making it a landmark for seamen navigating the waters around New York City. In early days, Darien's settlers largely ignored the land, as it was difficult to reach from the heart of town. But while it was, for the most part, a virgin parcel, the residents did clear it of trees to use the promontory as a space for cattle and other livestock to graze.

For a long time, the majority of Long Neck Point was owned solely by the Selleck family, who owned 125 uninterrupted acres of land on the peninsula, including holdings on some of the surrounding islands. Then, in 1836, Samuel Selleck divided a portion of the property among his six children in his will. This document, dated August 5, 1836, spelled the very beginning of Long Neck's transformation into a highly coveted area, home to beautiful and expansive estates the likes of which are rarely seen on American soil.

About thirty years after Selleck passed, the land changed hands once again, as it was bought by Harrison Olmsted, a direct descendant of Charlemagne who had amassed a fortune from business interests in transportation, including railroads and steamships. Olmsted owned the southern tip of the peninsula for seven years before selling it to Hugh W. Collender in 1872.

Collender was an Irishman who immigrated to the United States in 1850, beginning work as a skilled artisan making sashes and blinds. In time, he grew to be interested in manufacturing billiard tables, and by the end of his career, he was president of the Brunswick-Balke-Collender Company.

The Gilded Age on Connecticut's Gold Coast

A postcard picturing bathers taking in a beautiful day at Pear Tree Point Beach in Darien. *Photo courtesy of the* Darien News.

His introduction to the world of billiards took place in 1850, when he met another Irishman in America, Michael Phelan, who was known as the "father of billiards" in the States. Collender was a protégé of Phelan and eventually became his son-in-law after marrying Julia Phelan. A smart man with a brain equipped for science and engineering, Collender developed the "combination cushion"—a new kind of padding for pool tables that improved both ball movement and aesthetic—setting his billiard tables apart from the rest of the pack.

In 1860, Collender and Phelan coauthored the fifty-eight-page book *The Rise and Progress of the Game of Billiards*, which declared in its opening line that "not to be familiar with the game of billiards argues an imperfect education in the ways of the world, for it is a pastime which, whilst it promotes health from exercise and stimulates the mind."

The book provides further insight to just how significant Collender's combination cushion was to elevating billiards to a leisure activity that could be enjoyed by America's first class without creating a blight in their homes. "As late as 1854, the billiard table, which is now the graceful ornament of many a mansion, was a most unsightly construction," Collender and Phelan wrote. "The height of the cushions, the ungainly shape of the pocket irons, the yawning jaws and bristling sights, made what should be an ornament to a saloon or an apartment, a perfect eye-sore."

Collender built a home at the end of the point—which came to be known as Collender's Point in his time and for several decades thereafter—where he spent his summers until his death in 1890. In that time, he built several houses on his property and improved access to these homes by rearranging the roads. Originally, all the barns and outhouses situated on the point were positioned along its western shore so that waste could easily be disposed of in the sound, and the road clung to that shoreline. But Collender shifted the roads toward the center of the peninsula, where they remain today. With the roads thus situated, many homes constructed in this period boasted expansive backyards, as houses bordered the roads rather than the sea.

The point's beauty was greatly magnified during the years Collender called it home, as he took great pains to improve the landscaping and added masterful touches to the houses he erected, thanks in large part to the skilled woodworkers he employed at his five-story factory on Pacific Street in Stamford. The factory, which was built in 1873, employed roughly two hundred people at one point but lasted only a decade, burning to the ground on Valentine's Day 1883. While it was later rebuilt, operations were moved to another location shortly after its reincarnation.

In the 1879–80 edition of Stamford's directory, a description of the billiard factory declares that "the tables, as well as the various out fittings of the billiard room, manufactured by the Collender Co., are shipped to every civilized nation on the globe, and are the best known and most popular billiard manufactures in America."

When Collender died of kidney failure at his full-time residence on East Eighty-sixth Street, New York City, in 1890, several of his Collender's Point neighbors were identified as faces among the large crowd of mourners at his funeral in St. Patrick's Cathedral. John D. Crimmins, a new neighbor who had purchased a fifty-acre tract of land on the point from Collender earlier that year, was just one of these neighbors identified in a *New York Times* account of the funeral.

According to an entry in Crimmins's personal diary, recorded in 1891, he had spent several summers at the tip of the point, renting Collender's home for the summer season. He noted that "for seven seasons we occupied the house of the late Mr. Hugh W. Collender, and for six years that was known as the Mansion on the Point…and one year we occupied the house that is now Mr. O'Hara's."

It was during Crimmins's time living on the point that the area came to be known as one of the choicest spots of the entire Gold Coast; a 1913 map of Darien identified the stretch of land between Collender's Point and

The Gilded Age on Connecticut's Gold Coast

the new community of Tokeneke as "The Connecticut Riviera," thanks to its laundry list of high-profile residents. And Crimmins, an interesting and successful man during the late nineteenth century, was certainly one of the more prominent men on that list. He was a real estate developer who touched a great deal of projects in his native city of New York, where he also served as the parks commissioner for a time, as well as a financier and a philanthropist.

"During long years as a contractor, he played a material part in the physical upbuilding of this town and, some of the most memorable of its structures, particularly church edifices, rose stone upon stone under his guiding hand," the *New York Times* wrote of him after his death in 1917. "The success of his contracting business and the growth of his fortune carried him into the realms of finance, and he became as important a figure for a period in the economic life of the city as was he in its construction operation."

Crimmins brought his eye for beautiful buildings, which was well known in Manhattan, to Darien. There he constructed a summer house of his own on a fifteen-acre tract of land he had purchased from Collender for $32,500. His home, which stood regally on the property for more than 120 years before being razed in 2013, was a wooden masterpiece. With fourteen bedrooms and nine bathrooms, the three-story home, with turrets and peaks crowning its roofline, had ample room for the Crimmins family, which included eleven children.

In that 1891 diary entry, Crimmins lamented that "the progress of the building since has been tedious and the expense great, but in results, I think it will be satisfactory." And it was.

The custom floors, which were created by the craftsmen at Collender's billiard factory, zigzagged into intricately designed diamond patterns accented by three types of wood: oak, mahogany and walnut. The wainscoting and cove moldings decorated the entryway until the house's final days, turning the foyer into a time machine that transported visitors to Crimmins's day, when fires in the home's thirteen fireplaces roared with the force of the two stone lions guarding the estate's entryway from Long Neck Point Road. "The house is very comfortable and the furniture is new," Crimmins wrote in a separate diary entry, four days later.

Much of the splendor of the estate, which Crimmins dubbed Firwood after a plethora of fir trees growing on the grounds, lay outside the 9,900 square feet of living space. The lawn was expansive. With the house firmly planted just a couple yards from the street, there were hundreds of feet between it and the waterfront, where Crimmins built a long dock.

And the grounds were beautiful, with lush grass and a clear view of the sound. In 1894, Firwood served as the location for the picturesque wedding of Crimmins's eldest daughter, Susie Beatrix Crimmins, to Albert Gould Jennings, a Princeton graduate and a "leader in Brooklyn society" whose family also spent their summers on Long Neck.

"An orchestra, concealed behind ferns and flowers, played during the ceremony and at the banquet which followed," the *New York Times* reported, detailing the bride's dress, which was made of imported white silk and trimmed with duchess lace, as well as the "magnificent" diamond necklace Jennings had gifted her that day. "The house was handsomely decorated with flowers and plants."

In addition to the gorgeous flowers, grown in his greenhouse, Crimmins's grounds included another three acres purchased in 1904, creating room for a generous farm. "My garden looks plentiful," Crimmins wrote in 1891. "I have a farmer, a gardener, a man of all work and seven maid servants. In my stables are four horses for driving and two saddle horses. One for John and the other for Susie. We have three cows."

Crimmins was a man of the city, having been born in New York in 1844, yet he was well known for his interest in horticulture. According to the 1917 obituary in the *New York Times*, Crimmins stayed mostly out of politics, but he did earn the title of New York City Parks Commissioner, "due not to political ambition, but to his passion for flowers and for landscape gardening, a passion which led him to employ a score of gardeners at his country home in Noroton, Conn., where he cherished a collection of rare growths said to be worth more than $100,000."

Crimmins left a significant legacy, both in New York City—where homes he designed still line the streets, like his sixteen row houses between 222 and 252 East Sixty-eighth Street, and money he bequeathed continued to fund charitable ventures for years after his death—and in Darien, where subsequent generations of his family continued to call Long Neck Point home for more than a century.

While Long Neck Point served as a home for Collender and Crimmins, other corners of the town also attracted powerful businessmen, drawn to Darien's beautiful scenery and calm days.

Chapter 12
THE LEGACY OF WILLIAM ZIEGLER

A history of Darien during the Gilded Age would not be complete without mentioning William Ziegler, a man whose name can still be found around town in places like Ziegler's Cove, a summertime oasis for boaters coming from all over the area to seek out a quiet corner to moor up for an afternoon.

William Ziegler was born in 1843 near Pittsburgh to German parents. After his father's death, he moved to Iowa, where his mother and stepfather had purchased a farm. There, young Ziegler attended public schools before taking his first job as a printer's apprentice in a newspaper office. But his mind was better suited for science than for printing, and as a young adult, Ziegler shifted his focus, taking a job as a clerk at a pharmacy and studying telegraphy and chemistry.

In 1870, Ziegler joined forces with Joseph D. Hoagland and John H. Seal to form the Royal Chemical Company, which later became the Royal Baking Powder Company.

But tensions were high between Ziegler and his partners, and he left the company in 1888 after a drawn-out and bitter legal battle, selling his interest for $4 million. With that money, he purchased the Price Baking Powder Company and the Tartar Chemical Company to rebuild an empire of his own from scratch.

His business acumen led to his informal title as the "baking soda king." But he also made a name for himself as an explorer—or at least as a financer for explorers. In 1901, Ziegler became interested in polar exploration and

The Gilded Age on Connecticut's Gold Coast

The Ziegler family purchased a summer escape in Darien in 1902. *Photo courtesy of the Darien News.*

began his quest to earn the United States the honor of being the first nation to plant its flag in the North Pole. That year, Ziegler commissioned his first—unsuccessful—expedition, dubbing it "A Dash for the Pole." A second shot at the pole the following year also failed.

Later that same year, Ziegler purchased Darien's Great Island from the heirs of Daniel Edgar. The island, which is actually more of an arm off the eastern shores of Long Neck Point, included more than 170 acres of land but needed significant improvements. After his purchase, Ziegler set to work, drilling a well and harvesting rocks from a local ledge to use in building his massive house. The project was incredibly demanding, and at one point, Ziegler employed more than two hundred men to improve the property. The workers created an enviable estate, complete with a yacht basin, beach, mansion, outbuildings and a polo field.

Ziegler died in 1904 at the age of sixty-two, leaving behind a fortune valued at more than $370 million in today's dollars. The vast majority of the estate was left to his fourteen-year-old adopted son, William Ziegler Jr. The second Ziegler had been born the son of Ziegler's half brother and was adopted in 1896.

William Ziegler Jr. took up residency on Great Island during the summer months and continued to improve the property over the course of several years.

In 1927, Ziegler began a development, called Salem Straits, near his estates. Originally consisting of fifty-six acres of woodland situated along the jagged and rocky shorelines, Ziegler planned for and deeded out thirty-two plots, which shared the area along with a park and bathing beach for the residents.

Salem Straits was just one in a long line of residential developments that sprung up in Darien in the beginning of the twentieth century. As wealthy families searched for well-planned and enviable estates, they turned their attention to Darien, where thoughtful developers, like Ziegler and others, had created the exact type of neighborhoods they desired.

Chapter 13
TOKENEKE AND PLANNED DEVELOPMENT IN DARIEN

The Tokeneke residential park was established in Darien shortly after the turn of the century by three men: Joseph D. Sawyer (who had already successfully created an exclusive planned community called Hillcrest Manor in Greenwich, just west of the town's border with Stamford, in the 1880s), E. Hope Norton and Miner Davis Randall. Over the course of several years, the group cobbled together a cluster of several estates, creating the outline of the park, which grew to include more than 560 acres at its peak.

The name Tokeneke was chosen in honor of one of the local Native American chiefs whose name was among those mentioned in original deeds and titles between the Puritans and the Native Americans trading the land of Darien in the seventeenth century. "We don't know much about Tokeneke, the sachem," local historian Henry Jay Case wrote in a 1928 account of Tokeneke's history. "The white settlers around about here were apparently much more concerned in the extermination of the red man that they were in preserving his race for posterity."

Sawyer, Norton and Randall built a few homes on speculation to help lure wealthy buyers to the neighborhood, while other properties were sold with the condition that homes of a minimum value, which varied depending on the size of the lot, be constructed within a certain period of time. With plans to begin selling properties as soon as possible, the three men, who in 1901 formed the Tokeneke Corporation, built a twenty-five-room hotel, called the Tokeneke Inn, in 1904 with two very important goals.

THE GILDED AGE ON CONNECTICUT'S GOLD COAST

Stamford artist Whitman Bailey wrote the following about this picture he drew of Tokeneke in 1936: "Along the attractive shores of Tokeneke and within the Darien township, where great stone bulwarks jut into Long Island Sound and terraced gardens bask in the early Autumn sunlight, lies the locality of today's sketch." *Photo courtesy of the Stamford Advocate.*

In a 1987 "family album of the Tokeneke Club" commemorating the club's eightieth anniversary, Enid Oresman explained the motive: "The purpose of the Inn was not only to enable families to spend the summer in the country with the pleasures of the seashore, but as a place where prospective customers could live while selecting a home site and as a place to live during the construction of their houses."

With the hotel in place, the first land sale was recorded in 1905. But while the sales had begun, there were still significant hurdles in the corporation's way. Though several of the prime plots had direct water frontage, others were totally landlocked, posing a significant problem for marketing the properties. This inequality is aptly explained in the Corbin Document, a compilation of Darien town records put together in 1946 by former first selectman J. Benjamin Corbin: "The promoters found it difficult to get cottagers to buy without assurance of an accessible bathing beach that could be kept under control. It was therefore as much for the protection of the corporation as for the convenience of the cottagers that the Tokeneke Club was formed."

Transforming Greenwich, Stamford and Darien

As beautiful homes began springing up throughout Tokeneke, the park grabbed the attention of well-to-do buyers across the Northeast—and the press. In a July 1908 edition of *American Homes and Gardens*, writer Francis Durando Nichols swooned over Tokeneke, writing "it is delightfully situated on the Connecticut shore of Long Island Sound and is within close touch with railroad facilities. It comprises all the elements for the enjoyment of outdoor life, for it has miles of magnificent wooded drives, an inn for the accommodation of transient friends of the dwellers in the Park, a well-appointed casino, a garage and every convenience and form of recreation."

Homes cropped up throughout the residential park. The magazine piece points to several standout homes, including "Casa Del Point," which was one of the first houses constructed in Tokeneke. An article written by the same magazine a few months earlier detailed the charm of this home, owned by the same man who would buy Darien's Butlers Island a few years later. "One need spend no time in seeking the causes of the charm of this little house," the magazine wrote. "Its beauty speaks aloud on every side: in its form and silhouette, in the fine manner in which the solid stucco walls hold and retain the windows; in the roof, which so amply and obviously covers the building; in the grace and beauty of the subsidiary parts, the balustrades, the pergolas, the trellised window in the rear, the firm, strong entrance doorway, and, above all, in its delightful situation. A quiet, peaceful house this is, brooding serenely above a creek, with the deep waters of Long Island Sound in the not far distance."

The Tokeneke section of Darien on a beautiful summer day. The homes in this part of town were owned by prominent residents like Metropolitan Opera director Herbert Witherspoon, among others. *Photo courtesy of the* Darien News.

The Gilded Age on Connecticut's Gold Coast

In the coming years, prominent Americans like retired New York minister Reverend George F. Pentecost, famed organist Dr. Gerrit Smith and Herbert Witherspoon bought into the community. Witherspoon was a bass singer whose musical career took off shortly after his 1895 graduation from Yale University, where he'd been a member of the glee club. From humble beginnings, Witherspoon's talent brought him to the top of the world, as he became a recognizable name in New York City and across the globe. In November 1908, he made his debut at the Metropolitan Opera House, playing the role of Titurel in *Parsifal*. He received great acclaim and continued performing at the opera house regularly until 1916, appearing in the first American adaption of Tchaikovsky's *La Dama di Picche*, *Fidelio* and several other pieces in his tenure as principal basso. A tall man of six feet, two inches, Witherspoon was known for being kind, agreeable and unpretentious. "I've got a hard job to tackle before me as principal basso at the Metropolitan, but you may be sure I'll have a strong go at it," he told a journalist in 1908. "American singers are coming to the front by leaps and bounds, much faster than Europeans; but a good many fail because they wish to accomplish in two years what can only be done in eight."

After living his life on stage for so long, Witherspoon sought out peace and quiet in Tokeneke, buying the Tudor-style Shorewood home in the park in 1917. Prior to Witherspoon's ownership, Shorewood had been the summer home of E.H. Norton—one of the three Tokeneke founders—for a decade. Built of fieldstone near the base, with half-timber work and white plaster joining together for the façade, and topped with a red-shingled roof, Shorewood was reminiscent of an English manor house. And it fit well into the community's overall aesthetic; other homes, such as Joseph D. Sawyer's Hearthstone and Walter Blabson's home, were also designed in the half-timber style.

Later in life, Witherspoon became general manager at the Metropolitan Opera House, a role he played for just a short time before suffering a heart attack and dying in 1935.

Witherspoon wasn't the only notable American who found a private, peaceful retreat in the country at Tokeneke. Charles Lindbergh—the first pilot to cross the Atlantic Ocean in a solo, non-stop flight—purchased a home there in the 1960s. He stayed there until his death in 1974, and his wife, Anne Morrow Lindbergh, continued to live there even after his death, in a well-kept secret guarded by the sealed lips of their Tokeneke neighbors.

For more than a century now, Tokeneke has lived up to its stellar reputation, which *American Homes and Gardens* outlined in that 1908 article: "Truly a

Transforming Greenwich, Stamford and Darien

A postcard illustrating the Post Road in Darien shortly after the turn of the century. *Photo courtesy of the* Darien News.

summer residence park of singular beauty and enormous attractiveness. Hard indeed to please must be the country resident who can not find satisfaction and pleasure within its surroundings."

While the residential park of Tokeneke was by far the largest planned community in the town of Darien, it wasn't the only painstakingly planned neighborhood. Developments rose throughout town in the coming years, including the fifty-acre community built on Birch Road in 1922 that later grew to include another twenty acres, as well as the private, restricted park called Cedar Gate and the Delafield Estates. A year later, Hancock Lane, a forty-acre development off Middlesex Road, was purchased by Stoddard Hancock, the owner of New York's *Mail and Express*. While the property had at one point been home to shoe workers, Hancock developed it into a community of Colonial-style homes, each with gardens, fields and woodland on their parcel. Other developments included the 130-acre Allwood Lane community, which began in 1926, and Ridge Acres, begun in 1928 on a tract of land situated on Brookside Road.

One of the larger-scale planned communities to come to Darien in those decades was a development begun in 1926 on the western side of town, down in a peninsula bordering Holly Pond. The development was handled by Noroton Shores Inc., which hired about two dozen men from Baltimore to work around the clock for eleven months, dredging the area,

The Gilded Age on Connecticut's Gold Coast

In this undated rendering of homes along the shores of the Gold Coast, Stamford artist Whitman Bailey portrays old houses dreaming along the shore. *Photo courtesy of the Stamford Advocate.*

which includes what is now Nearwater Lane. In the process, the crew placed about 500,000 cubic yards of fill on the marshy land, increasing the possible development area by about fourteen acres. They laid roads, including Nearwater Lane, and built a 160-foot stone breakwater, creating an ideal setting for waterside retreats.

Chapter 14

THE DAY THAT DARIEN "ARRIVED"

As the beginning of the twentieth century chugged along, the very fabric of Darien shifted, something that was easy to see in many of the town's actions, including the 1913 Pageant of Darien, which took place near Gorham's Pond.

In 1913, a newly formed organization called the Women's Civic League had an idea. The group, which was made up mostly of wealthy wives of the town's most prominent gentlemen, decided to put on a pageant to showcase all the benefits of their small town. Pageants were a fashionable trend in 1913, and hundreds were thrown around the country.

In an article published in the *New York Times* in June 1913, William Chauncey Langdon, president of the American Pageant Association, described just how popular the trend had become. "North and South, East and West, from the cities and from the hay fields, from the mountains and from the seashore—everywhere—the word 'Pageant' is heard more and more every year and even every month," he wrote. "The ordinary bystander might well say, 'It is a craze!' And so it is. A sweeping enthusiasm is the characteristic quality of this new American craze for pageantry."

Unlike the modern understanding of pageants, which are often associated with beauty queens, tiaras and talent competitions, the pageants of the 1910s were elaborate performances with several acts designed to tell the tale of a town's past, present and future.

As Langdon wrote in 1913, "In America, the central type of pageant is the historical, as in England, the pageant that presents, in a series of dramatic

The Gilded Age on Connecticut's Gold Coast

A pen-and-ink sketch of Gorham's Pond during the summer of 1935 drawn by Stamford artist Whitman Bailey. *Courtesy of the* Stamford Advocate.

episodes, the past life of a town—with (as has been said) a tendency to continue the pageant drama down to the present. The modern pageant is drama in which the place is the hero and the development of the community the plot."

In Darien, the nine-episode pageant was scheduled to take place over the course of three days over Labor Day weekend. And it served as a defining time in the town, marking a pivotal moment when Darien first took center stage in Fairfield County. Thousands of people traveled into the town to see the festivities; while most were from nearby cities like Stamford and Norwalk, some historical accounts claim that people came from as far away as St. Louis to witness the pageant.

With Darien's most powerful women at the helm—as well as their husbands, whom they had enlisted to help with their efforts—the patrician part of town took the opportunity to literally rewrite the script for Darien's metamorphosis from a cluster of working farms into a coveted community for people of means and good taste.

The Women's Civic League (a precursor to the Darien Community Association) hired none other than Langdon himself to oversee the effort as master of the pageant and got to work planning the elaborate affair's nine episodes. With a budget of about $4,000 for each of the three days—a total budget of about $280,000 in today's dollars—no expense was spared to help put Darien on the map.

The pageant began with a heavily dramatized and romanticized introduction, in which a man and his family searched for a new place to call home, a place designed by a team of angels to provide them with rest and relaxation. In the performance, angels led him to that very place: Darien.

The first six episodes depicted significant historical moments in the town's past: the first English settlers in 1641, the 1670 war with Norwalk, the mill at the landing in 1740, the raid on Middlesex Church in 1781, Darien's official separation from the City of Stamford and incorporation in 1820 and the coming of the railroad in 1848–49.

From there, the episodes took on a new tone. In episode seven, townspeople depicted the beginning of Darien's transformation. Set in 1885, the episode's title was "Just Home," and it showed the trickling in of young men entering the country town, and others like it, spurring changes from the quiet, rural life of years past into a residential place with amenities customized for the men who brought progress to town on their heels. It also showcased the struggle of Darien's native residents, who saw the town not as a blank slate for progress to unfold but as "just home." This was followed by the eighth episode, "A Place in the Country," which was set in 1900. This act, transparently produced by Darien's newest residents, boasted of the luxurious and leisurely life Darien offered for these well-to-do city residents, searching for an angel's paradise of their own.

In episode nine, "The New Darien," the town leaped into the future, exploring Darien as the pageant's planners imagined it would be two years later, in 1915. An advertisement for the community's amenities and a figment of the summer families' imaginations that outlined a town built more for their pleasure than for the needs and wants of longtime Darienites, this episode touted the Darien of 1915 as an ideal place for newcomers to find a peaceful haven for relaxation in the country.

It was at that moment that two things became incredibly clear. Firstly, Darien's reins were in the hands of a small—but growing—number of wealthy families who came to the town first for summer retreats. Secondly, these families had big plans to permanently reshape Darien in ways that suited their wishes rather than the wishes of the town's oldest residents.

And it worked.

The Gilded Age on Connecticut's Gold Coast

In an article published in the *Advocate* that week, the newspaper declared that "Little Old Darien, that small neck of a town that has never done much except connect two large towns, arrived on Saturday. The vehicle was the Pageant of Darien. It was spectacular. It was splendid."

The moment that the newspaper touted as an important milestone for Darien was also significant for another reason. The prophecy outlined in the ninth episode, that of a wholesale change of the very fabric of the town, came soon—right on time. In the next couple years, Darien's transformation did indeed pick up, as the influence of families like the ones first depicted in episode seven continued to grow.

By 1915, the year imagined during the pageant, this new vision of Darien was already taking place. An inspection of town documents filed that year shows that the idea of Darien as a town of farmers and open fields was inching closer toward extinction, as the wealthy families who had first come to Darien in search for summer retreats increased their holdings across all corners of the town. In the 1915 grand list, the town's tax assessor recorded a total of 664 taxpayers, including 282 people who claimed a permanent residency somewhere other than Darien.

The grand list shows that the sum of Darien residents' estates was valued at $4,038,609, with non-residents' estates adding another $2,922,687. In addition, these out-of-towners who kept part-time estates in Darien accounted for 44 percent of landowners and held a combined 2,908 acres of land in town. Their average estate size was 10.1 acres, which was about 12 percent larger than the average resident's property, about 8.9 acres. Four residents claimed properties of more than 100 acres, compared with six non-residents, which included Helen Phelps Stokes's 228-acre estate and the Ziegler family's 170 acres.

This document, painstakingly recorded by hand and kept on file at the Darien Historical Society, shows the result of Darien's great transformation from a small town run by farmers to a lavish land of luxury, its destiny in the hands of wealthy newcomers.

Chapter 15

THE GOLD COAST TRANSFORMED

While the wholesale transformation of the once-agrarian communities into wealthy towns along the shore was mostly complete by the 1920s, the incremental changes in these towns did not end there. The large estates that sprung up around Fairfield County during the Gilded Age met significant changes in the twentieth century, as they were subdivided to make way for further development.

In the decade between 1946 and 1956, for instance, more than $100 million in construction was approved in the town of Greenwich alone. And these were not the typical American suburbs; zoning laws demanded large lots, with two- and four-acre zoning regulations in Greenwich's backcountry.

At the time of the 1950 census, the median value of a home in the Stamford metropolitan area was $15,638 ($148,926 in today's dollars)—a figure that was significantly higher than the state and national averages. By that time, the new Fairfield County image was firmly cemented as a white-collar life with all the trimmings. And that was reflected through a variety of factors. For example, census data shows that 3,375 residents of the Stamford metropolitan area worked in finance, more than twice the amount of residents working in the once-pervasive field of agriculture, an indicator that Wall Street life had thoroughly infiltrated and altered the state of suburban life in southwestern Connecticut. Additionally, annual median income was up to $4,127 per family, which was the highest in the state.

And those were just the averages. According to the *Greenwich Time*, mansions in the town of Greenwich sold for between $75,000 and $200,000

The Gilded Age on Connecticut's Gold Coast

(about $1.25 million to $3.34 million in today's dollars) during the 1940s. The paper also wrote that in 1948, one estate, named Beechcroft, marketed as "one of the finest of the Greenwich estates," sitting on thirty-two acres and boasting two ponds and a waterfall, went for $225,000—about fifteen times the already inflated Fairfield County average.

The lower corner of Connecticut containing Greenwich, Stamford and Darien had become synonymous with luxury, a fact that is best illustrated through a 1952 column published in London's *Daily Mail* newspaper, which declared that "it has become fashionable to live in Connecticut. To commute from the gilded super suburbs to one's New York office is to wear a smart snob label."

Notable residents made headlines on the regular throughout the twentieth century, including Ethel Skakel, a native of Greenwich's Lake Avenue who married future U.S. senator Robert F. Kennedy at Greenwich Avenue's St. Mary Roman Catholic Church, with his brother, future president John F. Kennedy serving as best man; Dorothy Hamill, the 1976 Olympic gold medalist in figure skating, who grew up in Riverside; baseball great Jackie Robinson, who moved to North Stamford after his Major League debut; and of course, Charles Lindbergh in Darien.

These days, celebrities are incredibly common in the area, with names like Gene Wilder in North Stamford, Mary Tyler Moore in Greenwich and New York Yankees GM Brian Cashman in Darien.

Of course, not every neighbor in these towns is a household name, but the legacy of wealthy residents has firmly embedded itself in the area, creating a corner of the country that is truly unique. In 2012, the median home values in the towns of Darien and Greenwich both totaled more than $1 million—the highest value the U.S. Census Bureau can record. In the same year, Stamford's was recorded as $514,900, a figure that (while lower than its neighbors) is roughly three times the national average.

The twenty-nine families who journeyed to Stamford from Wethersfield in 1641 would never have predicted that this area would become such a place when they first settled among the rocky shores and tall trees of Fairfield County. But a series of independent discoveries, fueled by the arrival of the railroad in 1848, created a seismic shift along the state's southwestern coastline, forever altering the destiny of the land that came to be known as Connecticut's Gold Coast.

Index

B

Benedict, Elias Cornelius 21, 29, 30, 31, 32, 33, 34, 35, 36, 37, 60

C

Carnegie, Andrew 55, 56, 57, 58, 60
casinos 41, 44, 92
Cedar Gate 117
Collender, Hugh W. 103, 104, 105, 106, 107
commuters 18, 43, 83, 93
Converse, Edmund C. 39, 65, 66, 68, 70
Conyers Farm 21, 39, 65, 72, 73
Crimmins, John D. 105, 106, 107

D

Delafield Estates 117

G

Greenway, Harriet Lauder 60, 61, 62
Greenway, James 60

I

Indian Harbor 23, 26, 28, 30, 31, 33, 35, 37, 60

K

Khakum Wood 59

L

Lindbergh, Anne Morrow 116
Lindbergh, Charles 116, 124
Long Neck Point 57, 58, 103, 106, 107, 110

N

Nearwater Lane 118

O

Old Greenwich 11, 19, 20, 44, 45, 48, 49, 50

P

Pageant of Darien 119, 121, 122

INDEX

R

Ridge Acres 117
Riverside 19, 20, 21, 124
Rockefeller, Percy 53, 54, 55, 56, 61
Rockefeller, William A. 51
Rockefeller, William G. 53, 54, 55, 56
Round Island 24, 44

S

Shippan 78, 79, 80, 81, 82, 83, 84, 85, 86, 87, 88, 90, 91, 92, 93, 94, 103
Sound Beach 19
Stamford factories 97, 99, 101, 105, 106
Stokes, Anson Phelps 57, 58, 88
Stokes, Helen Phelps 122
Stokes, Isaac Newton Phelps 58, 88
Stokes, James Graham Phelps 88

T

Tod, J. Kennedy 45, 46, 47
Tod's Point 47
Tokeneke 106, 113, 114, 115, 116, 117
Towne, Henry R. 97, 98
Tweed, William M. 23, 24, 25, 26, 27, 28, 29, 30, 32, 34

W

Wallack, John Lester 87, 88
Wallacks Point 88

Y

yacht clubs 30
Yale, Linus, Jr. 97, 98
Yale & Towne 97, 99, 101

About the Author

Maggie Gordon graduated from Syracuse University in 2008 with dual degrees in newspaper journalism and women's studies. Shortly after graduation, she moved to Fairfield County, Connecticut, to work as a reporter at the *Darien News*, a weekly newspaper in Darien. There, she covered everything from the school system to real estate and traffic before taking a job at the *Stamford Advocate* as the daily paper's education reporter. She worked as a schools reporter for a few years before launching the weekly feature "Trending with Maggie Gordon," which runs in the *Stamford Advocate*, *Connecticut Post*, *Danbury News-Times* and *Greenwich Time*. In addition to "Trending," Maggie also covers real estate in Greenwich for the *Greenwich Time*.

Courtesy of the Stamford Advocate.

Maggie lives in Stamford, Connecticut. While she's still a relative newcomer to the city, she plans to call Stamford home for a long time.

Visit us at
www.historypress.net

This title is also available as an e-book